Nicole Haring, Roberta Maierhofer, Barbara Ratzenböck (eds.)
Gender and Age/Aging in Popular Culture

The series is edited by Heike Hartung, Ulla Kriebernegg and Roberta Maierhofer.

Nicole Haring is a PhD candidate in English and American studies at the Center for Inter-American Studies at Universität Graz, Austria, with a DOC scholarship from the Austrian Academy of Sciences (ÖAW). Her fields of expertise are feminist theory and gender studies, US-American literature and cultural studies, Inter-American studies, and feminist pedagogy.

Roberta Maierhofer is a professor of American studies and Director of the Center for Inter-American Studies (C. IAS) at Universität Graz, Austria. She is a founding member of the European Network in Aging Studies (ENAS), supported the establishment of the North American Network in Aging Studies (NANAS), and has been a member of the Humanities and Arts Committee of the Gerontological Society of America. Her research focuses on American literature and cultural studies, gender studies, Transatlantic cooperation in education, and age/aging studies.

Barbara Ratzenböck is a sociologist and senior scientist at the Center for Inter-American Studies at Universität Graz, Austria. Her research and teaching focus on digitalization, gender, and generations, as well as Inter-American studies.

Nicole Haring, Roberta Maierhofer, Barbara Ratzenböck (eds.)

Gender and Age/Aging in Popular Culture

Representations in Film, Music, Literature, and Social Media

[transcript]

Funding: Published open-access with support of the County of Styria (Land Steiermark) and the Elisabeth-List-Fellowship Programme for Gender Studies of the University of Graz. This research was funded in part by the Austrian Science Fund (FWF) [I4187] as part of the MASCAGE project, which was funded by EU Gender Net Plus.

Bibliographic information published by the Deutsche Nationalbibliothek
The Deutsche Nationalbibliothek lists this publication in the Deutsche Nationalbibliografie; detailed bibliographic data are available in the Internet at http://dnb.d-nb.de

First published in 2023 by transcript Verlag, Bielefeld
© Nicole Haring, Roberta Maierhofer, Barbara Ratzenböck (eds.)

Cover layout: Maria Arndt, Bielefeld

Print-ISBN 978-3-8376-6242-9
PDF-ISBN 978-3-8394-6242-3
https://doi.org/10.14361/9783839462423
ISSN of series: 2702-7996
eISSN of series: 2702-8003

Contents

Introduction

Nicole Haring, Roberta Maierhofer, Barbara Ratzenböck

In her well-known book *Outlaw Culture: Resisting Representation* (1996), bell hooks acknowledges the critical analysis of popular culture as a "powerful way to share knowledge, in and outside the academy, across differences, in an oppositional and subversive way" (4–5). She demands to study and write about popular culture seriously as it is a terrain that is often conceptualized as "the culture of the masses" (Williams 1983, 237; Storey 2009, 10), and hence has great impact on societies. Following bell hooks' demand, this book has chosen popular culture as the context to engage with questions of representations with regard to gender, aging, and their intersectional identity markers.

Starting in the 1960s and 1970s, the analysis of popular culture became of great interest due to political and social movements across the globe paired with the development of mass media and technological advancements. In the humanities and the social sciences, influenced by Marxist scholars, the interest was particularly sparked by the growing awareness of the role popular culture plays in political mobilization. Additionally, new interpretive techniques emerged to make sense of forms of popular culture (Mukerji and Schudson 1989, 47). While all this was happening, scholars across disciplines wrestled, and still do so, with how to define popular culture. What does it encompass and where are its limits?

Raymond Williams (1983), who became famous as a pioneer of a 'broad' definition of culture, suggests four meanings of popular culture: "inferior kinds of works; works deliberately setting out to win favor; well-liked by many people; and culture actually made by the people for themselves" (237). Other scholars such as Harmon (1983) contributed to this definition by stating that it consists of "arts, rituals and events, myths and beliefs, and artifacts widely shared by a significant portion of group of people at a specific time" (4), whilst Mukerji and Schudson (1989) declared that "objects taken to be part of popular culture are readable objects, written or visual materials for which there are available traditions of interpretation and criticism" (48).

The definition of popular culture as an opposite of 'high-brow culture' stimulated postmodern ideas that no longer acknowledge a distinction between the two and soon popular culture was viewed as a "terrain marked by resistance and incorporation" (Storey 2009, 10). Linked to this development was the proposal of the concept of hegemony by the Italian Marxist thinker Antonio Gramsci (1949) with regard to the establishment of a political consensus where the dominant class's worldview is perceived as common sense. Within Gramsci's theoretical framework, popular culture is viewed as a distinct location for imagining radical change. Noteworthy here is also the ambivalent nature of popular culture. As a potential site for radical change, there is also always the remaining possibility to ultimately reestablish the status-quo which is temporarily challenged (Moody 2006, 173). Thus, when Stuart Hall (1986) remarked that "breaks, discontinuities, transformations, and asymmetry" (363) of popular culture are important for understanding its history, it is apparent that conceptualizing popular culture is a challenging task due to its nature as "a melting pot of confused and contradictory meanings" (Bennett 1980, 18).

As a theoretically contested area, popular culture encompasses numerous things and may be regarded as a vague contextual framework for analysis. However, our endeavor with this book aims at following a feminist analysis of popular culture that accepts the ambivalences of the terrain and regards them as a possibility to investigate its potential, as bell hooks would say, "as a powerful site for intervention, challenge, and change" (5). Following feminist popular culture scholarship, this book understands popular culture as a range of cultural texts which render meaning through images, words, and practices and thus include music, film, literature, and social media practices (hooks 1996; Moody 2006;

Milestone and Meyer 2011). We acknowledge popular culture as "a space of exchange between dominant and subordinate cultures" and aim at contributing to the wider debate over whether popular culture and its products "merely reflect society or act as part of the process of mediation in social life" (Moody 2006, 172).

Based on these premises, it is evident that popular culture plays a significant role in (re)producing social norms. This book focuses particular on representations of gender and ageing within popular culture. Similar to the distinction between sex and gender, age can be seen as biological, as well as socially constructed (Kontos 1999, 677; Maierhofer 2003, 26–27; Calasanti 2005, 9). The interconnectedness between gender and age has been evident since the 1990s, where recognizing age as a social construct would not have been possible without the introduction of race, class, and gender as categories of analysis in the decades before. Specifically, feminist theory determined the theoretical and methodological tools that led to the establishment of Age/Aging Studies as a field (Maierhofer 2019). In this context, Susan Sontag was among the first ones to address the particular intersection of gender and age at a conference of the Institute of Gerontology in 1973, when she identified the "Double Standard of Aging" as applied to men and women differently. In a feminist tradition, Sontag (1972) early on acknowledged aging as "a social judgement" of women rather "than a biological eventuality" (32).

Imbedded now in an intersectional feminist theoretical framework, highlighting the intersections of age and gender is merely a point of departure to pinpoint this particular cultural and societal interrelatedness while recognizing other intersecting identity markers, such as race, class, disabilities, sexual orientation, ethnicities, and origin, as well. With the establishment of intersectionality by Kimberlé Crenshaw in her legal discussion of Black women workers in the United States in 1989 and its introduction into different fields, a feminist framework has been established that is also useful for Age and Aging Studies to see identity categories as inherently relational. Hence, this publication aims at following Cho, Crenshaw, and McCall (2013), who argue that intersectionality was introduced as a "heuristic term to focus attention on the vexed dynamics of differences and the solidarities of sameness" to

expose how "single-axis thinking" (787) determines knowledge production and political and social systems. Since its origins, intersectionality
has been used in various forms, which nevertheless all aimed at problematizing and considering multiple dimensions of identity, including
race, class, gender(s), sexual orientation, dis/abilities, age, ethnicities,
religions, educational status, and geographical location.

Therefore, the chapters in this book address gender and aging in different spheres of popular culture, from film to music, literature, and social media. Problematizing the political dimension of popular culture
and its role in representing gender and aging is on the forefront of this
publication, where some articles address is explicitly and others subver-
sively.

Raquel Medina, in her chapter "Cinema and Glory: Almodóvar's Aging
Journey Through Space, Time, Pain, and Loss" convincingly sketches Pedro Almodóvar's 2019 film *Pain and Glory* as both, a story of male ageing
and representation of late creativity. In her analysis of the film, Medina focuses on the metaphorical journey of the ageing self of the main
protagonist who tries to create self-understanding by integrating contradictory biographical experiences into a narrative.

Also, **Leonor Acosta Bustamante**, in her contribution "Introspective
Conflict in the Middle of a Moveable Feast: The Tragedy of Ageing Masculinity in Paolo Sorrentino's *The Great Beauty* (2013)", explores cinematic
representations and negotiations of ageing masculinities. Closely examining Paolo Sorrentino's major hit, she traces how shots of the eternal city
of Rome and ruins of Roman Empire relate to and even represent the
film's protagonists own ageing. As Acosta Bustamante shows, the film
successfully links two opposing sets of sequences in narrating ambivalent experiences of male ageing: disengagement in terms of introspec-
tion and nostalgia of the main protagonist and images of constant social
engagement symbolized through intense partying.

Moving from powerful symbolic representations of intersections of
age and gender to illuminating lived experiences, **Shlomit Aharoni Lir
and Liat Ayalon** in their chapter examine power dynamics in the Israeli
film industry and how they relate to women film directors' positioning in

personal and historical time. For "The Celluloid Hurdles: Israeli Women Film Directors in the Prism of Gender and Time", Lir and Ayalon conducted a thematic analysis of 26 interviews with women film directors, as seen in the film "In the Director's Chair Sits a Woman" (2020) directed by Smadar Zamir. As the authors show, women in the Israeli film industry still face multi-faceted obstacles hindering their career development. As a result of their thorough analysis, Lir and Ayalon propose multiple powerful metaphors for understanding women directors' relationship to time in personal, professional, and historical contexts.

For her chapter, "'Be the Captain they remember' – Fandom Responses to Ageing Star Trek Protagonists", **Isabella Hesse** engaged in a virtual ethnography, conducting a qualitative analysis of posts in a Facebook fan group of the SF series *Star Trek: Picard*. In doing so, she explored fans' attitudes towards the ageing cast of the series. In addition to noteworthy differences in how male and female actors' ageing bodies were discussed online, she discovered that the notion of "ageing well" was central to fans' sense-making of the series. This was defined as actively embracing and integrating ageing into the performance, rather than denying it.

In addition to film and TV, contributors to this volume also explore how intersections of age and gender are represented in music. **Karen Fournier** analyses negotiations of female ageing in singer-songwriter Alanis Morisette's recent single "Reasons I Drink". Taking Helene Moglen's feminist concept of "transaging" as a starting point, she explores the idea of ageing as becoming, despite dysphoric experiences. As a chapter, "Gender, Rage, and Age in Alanis Morisette's 'Reasons I Drink'", critically examines gendered notions of youth and middle age and positions popular culture as a resource for alternative imaginaries of women's ageing.

In "On Being Silenced and Breaking Cycles – Deliberating Patters of Violence in Tori Amos' Works", **Melinda Niehus-Kettler** discusses personal and political negotiations of power, violence, and gender-based discrimination. Examining singer-songwriter Tori Amos' oeuvre, she explores processes of reclaiming power and voice, particularly of those who are more often silenced than others, including women and old people. In doing so, Niehus-Kettler positions music as a powerful tool of empowerment and community building.

Turning to the analysis of literary representations of gendered aging, **Nicole Haring** takes up Maierhofer's approach of "Anocriticism" in her reading of the contemporary novel *Girl, Woman, Other* (2019) by Bernadine Evaristo. In doing so, she thoroughly investigates and deconstructs cultural narratives of gender and age to highlight their socially constructed nature through an intersectional feminist lens.

Finally, **Marina Castelli Rosa** and **Mariana Lins** analyse the stereotype and meme of "tia do zap" ("WhatsApp aunt") prevalent in Brazil, which refers to older supporters of right-wing politicians. As they show, this gendered trope is used both by the left and the right for political agitation. In their contribution "'WhatsApp Aunts': Ageism, Sexism, and the Marginalisation of Older People in Brazilian Politics", Castelli and Lins highlight how this stereotype and meme is both ageist and sexist and hinders more reasonable debates across the political spectrum.

References

Bennett, Tony. "Popular Culture: A Teaching Object." Screen Education 34 (1980), 18: 17–30.

Calasanti, Toni. "Ageism, Gravity, and Gender." *Generations: Journal of the American Society on Aging* 29 (2005): 8–12.

Cho, Sumi, Kimberlé Crenshaw, and Leslie McCall. "Toward a field of intersectionality studies: Theory, applications, and praxis." *Signs* 38.4 (2013): 785–810.

Crenshaw, Kimberlé. "Demarginalizing the Intersection of Race and Sex: A Black Feminist Critique of Antidiscrimination Doctrine, Feminist Theory and Antiracist Politics." *University of Chicago Legal Forum* 1.8 (1989): 139–167.

Gramsci, Antonio. *Prison Notebooks*. Columbia: Columbia University Press, 1948.

Hall, Stuart. "Popular Culture and the State." *The Anthropology of the State: A Reader*. Ed. Akhil Gupta Aradhana Sharma. Maiden: Blackwell Publishing, 1989. 360–87.

Harmon, Gary L. "On the Nature and Functions of Popular Culture." *Studies in Popular Culture*, 6 (1983): 3–15.

hooks, bell. Outlaw Culture: Resisting Representations. London: Routledge, 1996.

Kontos, Pia C. "Local Biology: Bodies of Difference in Ageing Studies." *Ageing and Society* 19.6 (1999): 677–89.

Maierhofer, Roberta. "Feminism and Aging in Literature." *Encyclopedia of Gerontology and Population Aging*. Eds. Danan Gu and Matthew E. Dupre. Cham: Springer, 2019, 1–8.

Maierhofer, Roberta. *Salty Old Women: Eine anokritische Untersuchung zu Frauen, Altern und Identität in der amerikanischen Literatur*. Essen: Die blaue Eule, 2003.

Milestone, Katie, and Anneke Meyer. *Gender and Popular Culture*. Polity, 2011.

Moody, Nickianne. "Feminism and Popular Culture." *The Cambridge Companion to Feminist Literary Theory*. Ed. Ellen Rooney. Cambridge: Cambridge University Press, 2006. 172–91.

Mukerji, Chandra and Michael Schudson. "Popular Culture." *Annual Review of Sociology* 12 (1986): 47–66.

Sontag, Susan. "The Double Standard of Aging." *Saturday Review of The Society*, 23 September 1972. 29–38.

Storey, John. *Cultural Theory and Popular Culture: An Introduction*. London: Pearson Longman, 2009.

Williams, Raymond. *Keywords: A Vocabulary of Culture and Society*. Oxford: Oxford University Press, 1983.

Introspective Conflict in the Middle of a Moveable Feast
The Tragedy of Ageing Masculinity in Paolo Sorrentino's *The Great Beauty* (2013)

Leonor Acosta Bustamante

Abstract: *After being recognised as one of the most interesting filmmaker of post-millennial Italy in contemporary film studies, Paolo Sorrentino seems to lead the new Italian cinema as a proper auteur following the tradition of such important figures as Fellini, Rossellini, De Sica, Antonioni and Bertolucci. The Great Beauty, released in 2013, was his major hit and raised his career to an unthinkable level of fame and recognition in the international milieu. In his film, Sorrentino pays homage to Fellini's universe with some intertextual allusions to La dolce vita (1960), 8 $\frac{1}{2}$ (1963), and Roma (1972). However, this homage is not exempt from an ironic gaze about the excessive and grotesque landscape inherent to the eternal city; moreover, the old age of Rome explicitly displayed in interrupted shots of the ruins of the Roman Empire is symbolically related to the protagonist's awareness of his ageing. That the film's narrative starts with the celebration of his 65th birthday is nothing less than a meaningful hint, since it symbolically marks the age of retirement, physiological changes, and the starting point for the last phase in any man's life. It is the intention of this chapter to analyse the issue of ageing masculinity embodied in the male protagonist and expanded to the presentation of the decadent city of Rome as a technique for producing a film narrative consisting of two separate sets of sequences working together and constructing a short-circuit for the logics of the plot. Firstly, the protagonist's monologues are expressions about an introspective conflict, which defines male old age as a stage* *of contemplation, reveries, and nostalgia for the loss of youth, and, secondly, the insistent exhibition of social strident partying introduces a sense of psychological noise that conveys a sort of consolatory device, which unsuccessfully enough hides the reality of his self.*

Keywords: *Aging Masculinities; Paolo Sorrentino; The Great Beauty; Rome; Italian cinema; film narrative; cinematographic point of view; psychological process*

Introduction

The inclusion of Paolo Sorrentino in the Hall of Fame of Italian filmmakers is a phenomenon that possibly started some years ago, before the release of his greatly recognised movie *The Great Beauty* (2013), which won the Academy Awards for Best Foreign Language Film a year after. In 2014, he had attained the categorisation of an acclaimed figure within the realm of Italian culture of the 21st century, with the publication of three novels and the production of six movies including the one that is the object of analysis here. It is not difficult to understand that many film critics were aware of his increasing relevance in the international milieu, which provoked a rising interest in studying his career as the most significant author in Italian cinema since the golden age of Neorealism and Post-Neorealism. The highly stylised aesthetics of Sorrentino's films and his ironic comment developed along the lines of his scripts were the most interesting aspects for an increasing number of scholars, who started paying attention to this filmmaker as the proper emblem of an artist. It was in 2019 when this focalisation on Sorrentino's oeuvre reached the status of academic value, with the publication of a collection of articles entirely devoted to this director in the *Journal of Italian Cinema and Media Studies*. In the editorial, Annachiara Mariani elevated him to the consideration of a "transcultural and postnational" auteur and set the most highlighted components of his films in terms of formal, metaphysical and poetic grandeur:

Sorrentino's global breadth, his unique visionary style and distinctive aesthetics, his outspoken hubris and weighty poetics, his metaphysical lyricism and stunning compositions (with Luca Bigazzi behind the lens) tout court make him a contemporary director worthy of scrutiny. (Mariani 2019, 332)

Only two years after, two books on Sorrentino's career with the titles of *The Cinema of Paolo Sorrentino. Commitment to Style* (Killbourn 2020) and *Paolo Sorrentino's Cinema and Television* (Mariani 2021) consolidated the Neapolitan filmmaker and extended the diversification of research around his film narratives. In fact, some pieces of contemporary criticism stress the connection between Sorrentino's baroque style with inherent political statements, as Vito Zaggario (2016, 127) highlights in his chapter "The 'Great Beauty', or "Form Is Politics", where he states the intimate connection established between the complex visual style of Sorrentino's films and his engaged representation of Berlusconi's decadent Italy. That is also the thesis of Claudio Bisoni's chapter "Paolo Sorrentino: Between Engagement and *savoir faire*" (2016, 259), which comes to the conclusion that it is a common mistake to confuse his protagonists' perspective with that of the director's:

Sorrentino's cinema is rather read above all as a discussion that applies irony and contingency in turn to the world that it depicts on the screen. If this is the case, it is difficult to read any complicity between Sorrentino and the worlds of his characters. Instead he emerges, even before *Il divo*, as a director who creates pop icons that reflect [the collective Italian psyche. Italy as a space of solitude].

In particular, this collective Italian psyche was created by the Italian golden age of Neorealism and Post-Neorealism with the highly praised contributions of auteurs such as Federico Fellini, and Michelangelo Antonioni, who represented the profound decline of the bourgeoisie as metonymic of the nihilism invading the post-war era in Italy. The intertextual relations observed in Sorrentino's *The Great Beauty* and Federico Fellini's *La dolce vita* (1960) have been a matter of concern for many scholars (Carmelitano 2013; Lemus Polanía 2017; Durán Manso

2018; Mariani 2019; Mendieta Rodríguez 2019; Killbourn 2021), who determine the continuity of the 21st century film and the fictionalisation of Rome as the scenario of social and moral decline displayed by Fellini. Yet, the 2013 movie cannot be interpreted simply as a modern version of *La dolce vita*, mainly because it is not so easy to erase the fifty-three years that separate the two.

Carlo Celli and Marga Cottino-Jones (2007) define the 1960s as the moment in which Italian cinema took advantage of the total decay of Hollywood dominion caused by the disappearance of the studio system which controlled the production, distribution, and exhibition of movies for forty years. The period saw the increasing presence of Italian films in theatres, and, with it, the empowerment of Italian directors who were paving the way of differentiating their narratives from those of commercially driven American cinema. Besides, Italy became a perfect location to reactivate the taste for adventure films which was the origin of the "peplum" (movies about the ancient history of Rome), which led to the arriving of hundreds of cinema people at Rome. This influx of activity known as "Hollywood on the Tiber" offered many Italian technicians an opportunity to gain the experience and expertise essential to the boom in Italian film production in the 1960s (Celli and Cottino-Jones 2007, 86).

When Federico Fellini released *La dolce vita* in 1960, Italian cinema was ready to adopt the idea of artistic and experimental cinema in line with other national cinemas in Europe. By benefiting from the experience of Neorealist movies and their critical perspective about post-war Italy, the decade inaugurated a new form of seeing art cinema as a space for interrogating the economic boom of the period and its immoral consequences. The city of Rome embodied the perfect setting for the multiple sides of Italian society to be displayed throughout the psychological journey of the protagonist Marcello (Marcello Mastroianni), a journalist looking for stories to tell and a well-known inhabitant of the Roman nightlife. The narrative follows Marcello for one week through his psychological journey in his confrontation with his inner conflicts masked by the noisy party life of the city towards final self-assertion of not being able to gain any deep understanding of his superficial and empty self.

One year before, Michelangelo Antonioni had inaugurated his alienation trilogy with the release of *L'aventure* (1959), followed by *La notte* (1961) and *L'eclisse* (1962), three films that abandoned Rome for Milan in the second film in order to revise the most modern city of Italy as the place for moral unease and the breakdown of characters lost in a dense and out-of-focus society, hopeless in its own moral void. Antonioni's landscape transforms the city into a myriad of barren streets where the high buildings and the geometrical shots of blocks and small terraces reinforce the idea of claustrophobia. The characters present their unease by constantly moving from place to place, wandering without any possible end.

These two directors propelled Italian cinema to the level of the New Wave in France, the Free Cinema in Great Britain, and the New Cinema in Germany, to counterpart the Hollywood film industry and its dominion. They transformed the direct political criticism of Neorealism into a subtle denunciation of Italian social texture in times of economic boom and the consecration of neoliberal bourgeois life (Marrone 2016, 19). Moreover, what this group of films has in common is the tendency of representing social unease in the figure of a masculine type, that of the loser, producing representations of men who have lost their inspiration, the majority related to the realm of art: writers that have to succumb to the materialistic realm of gossip journalism leaving aside their transcendental desire of being literary masters, whose identity has lost the brilliance of the visionary and has reached a moment of delusion and despair. This existentialist nihilism entails an ageing process that is divorced from the effervescent youth and seems statically located in middle age as a new category of being, not just related to a proper evolution of life, but rather as a point in which they feel the weight of ageing and the abyss of not knowing how to go on. Antonioni's trilogy presents an enthralling excursion across a sentimental and social failure of bourgeois marriage as an imposition, an itinerary through the desert of love that the characters (male and female) see as an unbearable load. In this sense, there is no redemption, no solution for this state of mind, and their wanderings symbolise life, while the claustrophobic settings embody the hostility of a social order that abandons them to annihilation.

In general terms, the masculinity that all these protagonists perform is one with no safe sense of belonging in a world lacking opportunities, a social scenario obscured by their sterility (as non-fathers and as hopeless professionals), and their infructuous search for a stable self-identity. Along with the narratives, these male characters are bored with the women they have at their side, with their frivolous friends, and with a social texture they abhor. According to Sergio Rigoletto, the art cinema of post-Neorealist auteurs was proclaiming contemporary interrogations of manhood by showing male disempowerment and vulnerability. It meant the representation of the crisis of masculinity that in the next decade was going to concentrate on some of the most radical fictionalisations on sexual and social boundaries and their construction of acceptable and marginal male identities (Rigoletto 2014).

This is the connection between what Paolo Sorrentino offers with his acclaimed film *The Great Beauty* and the art cinema to which he wants to pay homage. Yet, the nation that was depicted in the 1960s is completely different from 21st century Italy, the political turmoil left by Silvio Berlusconi (Durán Manso 2018, 555; Picarelli 2015, 6) and the beginning of a period conditioned by the post-truth age, where the traditional borders between honesty and lying become completely blurred. Taking into account the very syntax of the film, the shot edition, the constant interconnection of images, and the surrealist collage of different camera angles and focuses, it is possible to understand how the film constructs a logical framework of action and themes concentrated on the omnipresent figure of Jep Gambardella, the main protagonist, and the need to read him in a problematic relation to Fellini's and Antonioni's dramatic universe.

Nonetheless, the development of this thematic interconnection conveys a contemporary reflection on the category of masculine identity and ageing, which is absent from the post-Neorealist filmmakers' interests. This aligns the film with prominent contributions in Masculinity Studies when this discipline turned to the issue of aging as part of its intersectional approach (Armengol 2018; Bartholomeaus and Tarrant 2016; Blundo and Estés 2005; Calasanti 2005; Calasanti and King 2005; Fennell and Davidson 2003; Hearn and Pringle 2006; Jackson 2016; Thompson 2018; Wangler 2013). Paolo Sorrentino's awareness of his protagonist's personal understanding of old age creates an important gap regarding the representation of masculinities in previous decades of Italian cinema, a strategy that allows him to interact with the principal achievements of Masculinity Studies mentioned above, evidently absent in his ancestors' films.

Rome as a Moveable Feast: Masculine Social Masks which Maintain the Dream of Youth

> Acting, like setting, constitutes a fundamental component of mise-en-scène and, also like setting, is shaped by other filmic elements such as camera angle and movement, lighting and editing. Rome's neighbourhoods, monuments and landmarks are narrative spaces that have loaned themselves to myriad interpretations: historical, ideological, psychological and symbolic. (Cooper 2017, 263)

Taking as a metaphor the title of Ernest Hemingway's memoirs (*A Moveable Feast*, published posthumously in 1964), and concentrating on the idea of an eternal city, Paris, as the scenario of the writer's diverse experiences in a foreign and revolutionary country devoted to the arts as the political engine of the times in the decades of his coming of adulthood, it is possible to make a connection between this symbolic city and the Rome fictionalised in *The Great Beauty* by Sorrentino. If Paris was the capital of the avant-garde, of the attack against classicism and the bourgeois manners, and of the liberation of the senses for the sake of innovation and rupture, the Rome represented in Sorrentino's film embodies the failure of this infinite hope that Paris represented one century ago.

Besides, the city shown in *La dolce vita* situates Rome in the late 1950s, when it was a famous tourist destination and the European capital of Hollywood crews: a cosmopolitan, sophisticated, and frivolous city invaded by rich foreigners for the true Italian citizens to take economic advantage of. This is why Fellini selects the settings with the objective of being recognised by all spectators: the dome of St. Peter's Basilica, Bernini's Columns, Trevi Fountain, and Via Veneto, compounding an image of grandeur and monumental splendour. However, Sorrentino's depiction of Rome takes a significant turn, and apart from the Coliseum (which stands for the B-side of Gambardella's terrace), the buildings chosen to establish the connection with the past transform previous grandeur into a cynical perspective, by which the touristic postcard turns into intricate associations with the characters' inner desolation, usually taking the interior of phantasmagorical palaces under candle-light and plunged into silence. As Luigi Carmelitano (2014, 157) asserts, Roma in *The Great Beauty* is the metaphor of paralysis, an immoveable city that is incapable of coping with the present, passively witnessing its decadence while being consoled with the remembrance of its imperial past.

The opening scene reveals Sorrentino's perspective regarding this idea: Rome's splendour has some effect only in admiring tourists that can even collapse as victims of a sublime experience, as it happens with the Japanese man sighting the city from the Janiculum, the eight hill of the capital. This overture introduces a list of film techniques that are going to set the baroque composition, the complexity of symbols, and the intertextual games all along with the narrative. In the published script of the film, the scene is described with incredible minute detail: the image of a cannon starts a quick syntax of travelling shots depicting the Janiculum as a place of mixing categories: the spectators of the can-non firing, the Japanese tourists, the workers, the aristocratic woman smoking, the choir singing David Lang's "I Lie" (a song released in 2013 but still keeping the tone of antique sacred music) inside the monu-mental building, while the camera shows the Garibaldi statue and fixes its attention on the words 'Roma or death' (Sorrentino and Contarello 2013).[1] The transcendental effect on the spectator is counteracted by the tourist's fainting and the tourist female guide's lack of empathy ('Oh, my Asian man has died', Sorrentino and Contarello 2013), and the script finishes this scene with the words: 'And the last shot is for Rome, mon-

---

umental and most beautiful. And heartless' (Sorrentino and Contarello 2013).

The lack of emotion invades the rest of the Roman scenarios from this beginning to the end of the movie, and it is what joins the category of 'city as background' to that of 'city as a character', taking the thesis at the core of Carla Molinari's contribution, "The Urban Dimension as Film Character: Rome in *The Great Beauty*" (2021). The link between the two categories is clearly the protagonist, Jep Gambardella, who permeates the plot with his cynical perspective, and who sets the structure of the thematic lines connected with all Roman scenarios.

The Roman settings introduced in the film produce a thematic structure which divide the plot into several sections regarding the different meanings of the social gatherings represented: the birthday party, Jep Gambardella's terrace in front of the Coliseum, monuments as the containers of postmodern art, streets and places as frames of the protagonist's wanderings. All of them function as metaphor of the old age of the eternal city in intimate connection with the ageing Gambardella, who constantly tries to retain the spirit of youth symbolised by his brilliant, colourful suits, and his intense countenance. The social success of the protagonist is concerned with the arresting power of surfaces, just like Rome, whose beauty wastes away before the eye. (Picarelli 2015, 8)

It is not by accident that the second scene of the film takes his bizarre, noisy, and appealing 65th birthday party to a hotel terrace, where his ageing male friends perform their lost adolescence in a quite ridiculous manner in the middle of the turmoil of young, sexy bodies. It is full of significance that Sorrentino's selection of film techniques produces a collage of different shots to stop in a moment and divorce Gambardella from the rest, the former looking directly at the camera and saying that he loves the smell of the old people's houses. With this intrusion of the protagonist's interior monologue, Sorrentino offers clues to understanding the doubling of his character: on the one hand, the successful still-appealing man of the world, the one invited to all parties in Rome, the outside performance of the once-famous writer, and, on the other, the inner side of old age, the recognition of his life coming to a phase of decline, in sum, the protagonist of Fellini's film waving goodbye to middle-age (Lemus Polanía 2017, 29).

Actually, as Molinari demonstrates, in Sorrentino's film "Rome is not really explored as a whole city" (2021, 129), but as compendium of individual sites forming a collage of experiences associated with Jep Gambardella's social position in the bourgeois, decadent community he belongs to. Among these, there is special insight in the meetings with friends at his terrace, a repeated setting that punctuates the narrative with the constant take of the Coliseum as a bored witness of these conversations dipped in alcohol and exhausted by rivalry, greed, and envy. The protagonist's narrative voice is used to deepen each secondary character's psychological profile, normally expressed by means of confrontations around the political situation of Rome, the anti-essentialism of culture, and the criticism of the Church. Politics, culture, and Catholicism are the objects of satirical comments juxtaposed by some scenes exploring the superficiality of all. To convey this idea, there are spectacular moments in which Gambardella, playing the role of the interviewer of important characters, assists to art forms, such as the one represented in the Antique Roman Aqueduct with a female artist totally naked and with her pubic hair dyed in red with the communist flag drawn on her pubis. Her only line states 'I do not love you at all' (Sorrentino and Contarello 2013), while she precipitates against the aqueduct stones and faints with blood emanating from her head. In a sense, this is the state of affairs with culture and art in Sorrentino's film: the relativism of postmodern art at the service of politics without any effect on the spectator, but with the enthralling presence of Imperial Rome as the stage.

Within these meetings, there is one that seems to establish a strong line of thought in *The Great Beauty* with respect to the Catholic Church and Rome as the site of the Pope, something that again connects with Fellini's oeuvre. The series of scenes associated with this issue comes in the last part of the film and has to do with the arrival of Sister Maria the Saint, a sardonic recreation of Saint Teresa of Calcutta, who is visiting Rome as part of a religious tour accompanied by a manager. Jep Gambardella is asked to interview her but she rejects, accepting in the course of events to share dinner at the journalist's home. This female character, as old as the city, grotesque in her physical weakness, toothless and completely wrinkled, with feet that cannot touch the ground when sitting on any chair, provokes a short-circuited situation when having dinner with Gambardella's friends. Poverty and silence do not form part of their character, and the Saint imposes a psychologically tense atmosphere on them. She is part of another world, an alien in the palace inhabited by the journalist, yet she does not seem to be aware of the shock she produces in the group when her manager pronounces her age: 104 years old, or when he says what she eats everyday: 40 grams of roots. When the group dissolves in the middle of the night, Sister Maria has disappeared and Gambardella finds her sleeping on his study's floor, in a manner that provides a link with the protagonist's assimilation to ageing. In this line of interpretation, Gambardella is again young regarding the emaciated woman who can live of nothing, and the Saint is transformed within the plot into a sort of oracle (imaginary or real, it does not matter) for the 65-year-old man. This is why the most intense and brief dialogue takes place at dawn when the protagonist wakes up and goes to the habitually crowded terrace, to meet the woman surrounded by hundreds of flamingos that seem to have some sort of communication with the Saint. Astonished by the image, Gambardella keeps silent while Sister Maria asks him why he did not write a second book, to which he answers: 'I searched for the great beauty but I did not find it' (Sorrentino and Contarello 2013). And finally, in one of the scenes that construct the emotional ending of the film, the old woman says: 'Do you know why I eat only roots? [...] Because roots are the most important' (Sorrentino and Contarello 2013).

Introspective Insights: Gambardella's Revelations About the Ache of Ageing

Sorrentino's films are character driven: without exception, the protagonist's vision of the world and his impact on or clash with the surrounding human community is central. Every main character is the *divo*, the main attraction of his world. Yet the protagonists are often relatively detached, if not entirely marginalised, from the communities that revolve around them. (Bisoni 2016, 255)

Extending this idea with the category of masculinity in mind, it is possible to say that Sorrentino's films are driven by different performances of Alpha male protagonists who need to cope with the strict codes of gender as imperative to maintain popular admiration. The focus on characters suffering from masculine defects positions the narrative within a very contemporary issue around the construction of gender. That human beings not only have bodies but that they *are* bodies is a consideration of the social construction of human corporeality and of the cultural regulation imposed on it. The body, from this perspective, must be understood as subject (the physical embodiment of a self, the site of subjectivity, the container of the mind) and object (the most intimate and primal property, the material part that is categorised and conditioned by social and cultural norms). In line with constructivist theories about identity and the relevance of understanding the body as the site of power inscription, Nick Crossley (2006) considers that the perception of this problematic duality transforms embodiment into a reflexive process, which Paolo Sorrentino uses in *The Great Beauty* to explore the protagonist's conflict between "the experience of being and having [a body that was young] and irony and nostalgia [when embodying old age]" (Simor and Sorfa 2017, 6).

In the previous section, I have been arguing that the presence of Rome does not take the function of providing a background setting but rather is used as a psychological space for Gambardella's display of his social mask. In spite of the first impressions, there are many more scenes devoted to investigating what the protagonist's mask hides in his interior, reinforced by the multiple sequences filmed inside houses, palaces, and monuments. Besides, the plot does not follow a simplistic timeline with action at the service of the film syntax; as explained above, the techniques used by Paolo Sorrentino are meant to show different experiences of the leading character not necessarily linked with a linear narration. As Ponce Beniuc (2018, 187) explains, the story becomes a set of disjointed actions where there is no possible differentiation between the trivial and the relevant, between the subjective and the objective, the imaginary and the real.

What is evident is that the formal elements included in order to reveal Gambardella's thoughts produce a doubling in the film style: the noisy world of the protagonist's social appearances contrasts with the calm dialogues he maintains in the intimacy and the intrusive monologues that he pronounces addressing the spectator while sound, music, and action stop. Regarding these scenes, the most relevant topics explored about Gambardella's inner self consist of two main axes related to ageing: on the one hand, the need to situate sexuality at a different level of experience unconnected with the sense of the present, and, on the other, the imperative of equalling old age with a period of loss, a phase of nostalgia (Killbourn 2020, 86–90) which guides him sometimes to pessimism and nihilistic feelings.

Within these sections, Sorrentino makes room for the characterisation of secondary characters that accompany the protagonist on this journey of the self, with manifest differences between male and female companions. The most highlighted male figure that functions in this manner is Gambardella's close friend Romano, a failed playwright and a failed lover of a young actress that despises him whenever she has the opportunity. In the conversations they maintained at Romano's small department and at Gambardella's luxurious place, the protagonist shows the impossibility of returning to his golden age as a reputed writer while sharing experiences of youth in their natal provinces far away from Rome. In their last meeting, Gambardella has been talking to a magician, Arturo, who is able to make a giraffe disappear, the protagonist then asks 'Can you make me disappear?', and the magician answers 'If I really could make someone disappear, would I still be here, at my age?' (Sorrentino and Contarello 2013). After this pessimistic comment, Romano appears and tells his friend that he is going back to his natal town: 'Roma has disappointed me' (Sorrentino and Contarello 2013), and Gambardella looks at him with a mixture of sadness and recognition, as if wanting to be like him, with no social load, free to go and find the roots of his identity. In a sense, to lose his friend in Rome means to lose any emotional link with his past, and so, to break all options to come back to his youth.

In terms of a re-situation of sexuality, Gambardella's social mask conveys an image of sex appealing in the display of flirting and seducing women as all sequences dealing with partying constantly show. The lack of emotional empathy is inherent to Gambardella's social performance, but it also conditions his hidden self, something that seems to reinforce his sense of solitude and dullness. When facing his life after his 65th birthday, he is unable to find a true emotional response, since it seems that his social mask has been muting this vital experience when there was no need for it. Yet he starts obliging himself to the construction of several intimate relations to taste life in a different manner. This is the case of Ramona, whom he meets at a striptease club in Via Veneto, being the 40-year-old daughter of one of Gambardella's friends and one of the oldest strippers at the club. Ramona is the protagonist's female alter ego, a woman with no interest in creating a family of her own, but with an ageing body that might ruin her life, not only in terms of her economic maintenance but mainly because her body's erotic exposure is the most important part of herself. In finishing the scene, the protagonist and Ramona are left alone talking about the future, and Gambardella confesses. 'I feel old' and she answers, 'You are not young' with a smile on her face (Sorrentino and Contarello 2013). This brief dialogue introduces an epiphanic moment in Gambardella's inner process of recognition and this is perhaps why he starts a relationship with her that ends apparently with Ramona's death in his bedroom. The scene follows one in which she is assaulted and receives a supposedly fatal blow when they were coming back from an art performance. The camera focuses on the splendid body of the stripper semi-naked on the bed, seemingly sleeping after a convulsive night, he is preparing breakfast and notices that something is wrong with Ramona, then he says 'It has been a good chance not to have sex this night', she smiles; and when breakfast is ready he approaches her touching her weakened body, then shares with her a repeated imaginary scene with her at the moment in which he decides to lay next her in bed: 'Can you see the sea?', 'Where?' she asks, 'In the ceiling', 'I see it, the sea' (Sorrentino and Contarello 2013). By sharing this emotional moment, the couple seems to be in complete connection, but the film wants to destroy the possibility of rebirth for Gambardella in the instant Ramona is dead.

Another important point in relation to the remembrance of transcendental moments is the introspective take about his first love affair before establishing in Rome with Elisa. As a conventional adolescent experience, love is mixed up with sensuality, symbolised by the presence of the sea at night, and sexual attraction. Elisa is a character depicted only through the protagonist's perspective by means of the nostalgic moments in which he quits his social masks and imagines the sea in his ceiling. The repeated scene is that of an adolescent girl silently conquering the heart and the libido of the protagonist in his youth: the sequence at night near the sea constructs this instant in the loneliness of a natural landscape, letting the spectator know that there was no sexual contact, but an experience of a lost opportunity. In the middle of the plot, a man called Alfredo waits for him at his door to inform him about Elisa's death, the arrogant Gambardella feels the pinch of learning that his idealist love has disappeared, even more upset when Alfredo confesses that Elisa has been loving him for all her life. This apparently introduces an emotional element to save the protagonist from the moral decay he has made of his life, and this idea is reinforced when Sister Maria refers to the importance of roots. Sorrentino makes the spectator think that this is the great beauty Jep Gambardella has been looking for:

> When Jep realises that 'the great beauty' he was looking for was his love for Elisa (Annaluisa Capasa), he is able to create art again and he starts writing a novel about this revelation. Thanks to the final scene's overtly stylized representation, this revelation also becomes ridiculously absurd. (Simor and Sorfa 2017, 11)

Jep Gambardella has along with the narrative many ways of recovering this final beauty he is constantly searching for as an existential motif, but he is so conditioned by his bourgeois life in Rome and by the comfortability of wearing the mask of a man of power, that all opportunities are just brief moments of nostalgia that in few seconds are forgotten. There is no love affair, no professional chance, no friendly gesture that can move the divine Gambardella to abandon his constructed self, since finally, he is what the Roman bourgeoisie has made of him. With nothing to do with beauty, the final sequence serves as the ironic comment on the whole narrative. There is no possibility of grasping the splendour of the past, there is only the need to forget and go to the eternal hypocritical party in the very sense that Federico Fellini and Michelangelo Antonioni depicted the problems of masculinity four decades before, only with a postmodern touch. (Mendieta Rodríguez 2019, 336)

References

8 $\frac{1}{2}$ *(Otto e metzo)*. Dir. Federico Fellini. Narrs. Tullio Pinelli, Federico Fellini, Ennio Flaiano, and Brunello Rondi. Cineriz, Francinex, 1963.

Armengol Josep. "Aging as Emasculation? Rethinking Aging Masculinities in Contemporary U.S. Fiction". *Critique: Studies in Contemporary Fiction* 59.3 (2018): 355–367, 10.1080/00111619.2017.1386157

Bartholomeaus, Claire, and Anna Tarrant. "Masculinities at the Margins of 'Middle Adulthood': What a Consideration of Young Age and Old Age Offers Masculinities Theorizing". *Men and Masculinities* 19.4 (2016): 351–369.

Bisoni, Claudio. "Paolo Sorrentino: Between Engagement and *savoir faire*". *Italian Political Cinema. Public Life, Imaginary, and Identity in Contemporary Italian Film*. Eds. Giancarlo Lombardi and Cristian Uva. Oxford: Peter Lang, 2016. 251–262.

Blundo, Robert, and Tamara Estés. "The Peculiarities of Men Aging: A Collection of Anecdotes". *Journal of Sociology and Social Welfare*, 32.1 (2005): 61–70.

Calasanti, Toni, and Neal King. "Firming the Floppy Penis. Age, Class, and Gender Relations in the Lives of Old Men". *Men and Masculinities* 8.1 (2005): 3–23.

Calasanti, Toni. "Ageism, Gravity, and Gender: Experiences of Aging Bodies". *Generations* 29.3 (2005): 8–12.

Carmelitano, Luigi. "Roma en la película La grade belleza de Paolo So-rrentino". *Ángulo Recto. Revista de estudios sobre la ciudad como espacio plural* 6.1 (2014): 157–160.

Celli, Carlo, and Marga Cottino-Jones. *A New Guide to Italian Cinema*. New York: Palgrave-Macmillan, 2007.

Cooper, Allison. "Performing Rome". *The Italianist* 37.2 (2017): 263–267. https://doi.org/10.1080/02614340.2017.1332719

Crossley, Nick. *Reflexive Embodiment in Contemporary Society*. Berkshire, UK: Open University Press, 2006.

Durán Manso, Valeriano. "La ciudad de Roma como imagen de marca en el cine: presencia y evolución". In *Vacaciones en Roma, La Dolce Vita y La Gran Belleza".¿Qué es el cine?* Ed. Mercedes Miguel Borrás. Valladolid: Ediciones Universidad de Valladolid, 2018. 547–558.

Fennell, Graham, and Kate Davidson. "'The Invisible Man?' Older Men in Modern Society". *Ageing International* 28.4 (2003): 315–325.

Galt, Rosalind, and Karl Schoonover. *Global Art Cinema: New Theories and Histories*. New York: Oxford University Press, 2010.

Hearn, Jeff, and Keith Pringle. *European perspectives on men and masculin-ities: National and transnational approaches*. Basingstoke, UK: Palgrave Macmillan, Basingstoke, 2006.

Jackson, David. *Exploring Aging Masculinities. The Body, Sexuality and Social Lives*. Basingstoke, UK: Palgrave Macmillan, 2016.

Killbourn, Russell. *The Cinema of Paolo Sorrentino. Commitment to Style*. New York: Columbia University Press, 2020.

Kriebernegg, Ulla, and Roberta Maierhofer, editors. *The Age of Life. Living and Aging in Conflict?* Bielefeld: transcript. Aging Studies, 2013.

L'avventura. Dir. Michelangelo Antonioni. Narrs. Tonino Guerra, Miche-langelo Antonioni, and Elio Bartolini. Cino del Duca P.C, Produzioni Cinematografiche Europee (P.C.E.), Société Cinematographique Ly-re, 1960.

L'eclisse. Dir. Michelangelo Antonioni. Narrs. Tonino Guerra, Michelan-gelo Antonioni, and Elio Bartolini. Cineriz, Interopa Film, Paris-Films Productions, 1962.

La dolce vita. Dir. Federico Fellini. Narrs. Federico Fellini, Tullio Pinelli, Ennio Flaiano, and Brunello Rondi. Pathé Consortium Cinéma (P.A.C.), Riama Film, Gray-Film, 1960.

La notte. Dir. Michelangelo Antonioni. Narrs. Tonino Guerra, Michelangelo Antonioni, and Ennio Flaiano. Nep Films, Silver Films, Sofitedip, 1961.

Lemus Polanía, Juan Carlos. "*La grande bellezza, La dolce vita* en technicolor". *Ventana indiscreta* 18 (2017): 26–31.

Lombardi, Giancarlo, and Cristian Uva, editors. *Italian Political Cinema. Public Life, Imaginary, and Identity in Contemporary Italian Film*. Oxford: Peter Lang, 2016.

Mariani, Annachiara, editor. *Paolo Sorrentino's Cinema and Television*. Bristol, UK; Intellect, The University of Chicago Press, 2021.

Mariani, Annachiara. "Paolo Sorrentino: A Transcultural and Post-national Auteur". *Journal of Italian Cinema and Media Studies* 5.3 (2019): 331–338.

Marrone, Gaetana. "Italian Political Cinema. The Early Masters". *Italian Political Cinema. Public Life, Imaginary, and Identity in Contemporary Italian Film*. Eds. Giancarlo Lombardi and Cristian Uva. Oxford: Peter Lang, 2016. 17–30.

Mendieta Rodríguez, Elios. "El tedio irónico en el sujeto contemporáneo. Estudio del *ennui* en *La grande belleza* (Paolo Sorrentino, 2013)". *Escritura e Imagen* 15 (2019): 323–343.

Molinari, Carla. "The Urban Dimension as Film Character: Roma in *The Great Beauty*". In *Paolo Sorrentino's Cinema and Television*. Ed. Annachiara Mariani. Bristol, UK: Intellect, The University of Chicago Press, 2021. 109–136.

Picarelli, Enrica. "*The Great Beauty*: Italy's Inertia and Neo-baroque Aestheticism HYPERLINK "https://doi.org/10.18573/j.2015.10032"". *JOMEC Journal. Journalism, Media and Cultural Studies* 8 (2015). https://doi.org/10.18573/j.2015.10032

Ponce Beniuc, Sylvia. "Pablo Sorrentino. Creer y hacer creer en el mundo". *AURA. Revista de Historia y Teoría del Arte* 8 (2018): 183–196.

Rigoletto, Sergio. *Masculinity and Italian Cinema: Sexual Politics, Social Conflict and Male Crisis in the 1970s*. Edinburgh: Edinburgh University Press, 2014.

Roma. Dir. Federico Fellini. Narrs. Federico Fellini and Bernardino Zapponi. Ultra Film, Les Productions Artistes Associes, 1972.

Simor, Eszter, and David Sorfa. "Irony, Sexism and Magic in Paolo Sorrentino's Films". *Studies in European Cinema* 14.3 (2017): 200–215. http s://doi.org/10.1080/17411548.2017.1386368.

Sorrentino, Paolo, and Umberto Contarello. *La grande belleza*. Milan: Skira editore, 2013.

Sorrentino, Paolo. *La grande belleza. Diario del Film*. Milan: Varia/Feltrinelli, 2013.

The Great Beauty. Dir. Paolo Sorrentino. Narrs. Paolo Sorrentino and Umberto Contarello. Indigo Film, Medusa Produzione, Pathé, France 2 Cinema, Babe Film, Canal+, Mediaset, 2013.

Thompson, Edward H. Jr. *Men, Masculinities, and Aging. The Gendered Lives of Older Men*. Lanham, Maryland: Rowman and Littlefield Publishers, 2018.

Wangler, Julian. "Representation of Old Age in Media. Fear of Aging or Cult of Youth?". In *The Age of Life. Living and Aging in Conflict?* Eds. Ulla Kriebernegg and Roberta Maierhofer. Bielefeld: transcript. Aging Studies, 2013. 17–20.

Zagarrio, Vito. "The 'Great Beauty', or Form Is Politics". *Italian Political Cinema. Public Life, Imaginary, and Identity in Contemporary Italian Film*. Eds. Giancarlo Lombardi and Cristian Uva. Oxford: Peter Lang, 2016. 119–130.

Cinema and Glory
Almodóvar's Aging Journey Through Space, Time, Pain, and Loss

Raquel Medina

Abstract: *This chapter analyses Pedro Almodóvar's 2019 Pain and Glory as a metaphorical journey of the ageing self. This journey follows the concept of ageing as illness and decline thus triggering the nostalgic act of remembering and recreating an irrecoverable past to overcome the nearness of death. By describing his passage from midlife (crisis) to the third age as the accumulation of ailments and the lack of sexual desire, the protagonist, Salvador Mallo, follows the medicalization of old age. It is only through heroin and cinema that he can get rid of the pain he feels and can 'return' to his own 'happy' past. The idealization of his (lost) childhood in the poor rural Spain of the early 50s is recreated using bright colours and happy songs and the figure of the mother. In opposition, Salvador's move to Madrid in the 80s is not directly presented on screen. His life there is recalled through two male figures who reappear in the present: Alberto (the star of his film Sabor) and Federico (Salvador's lover in the 80s). The Madrid of the 80s is indirectly depicted through Salvador's play (Adicción) and film Sabor as both the epicentre of Spanish creativity and homosexuality, but also as the space in which drugs killed and destroyed the lives of many. Finally, this study shows how late-life creativity in the film is conceived as a time for recycling memories, and the film itself as the space for recycling Salvador's earlier films to display his global glory.*

Keywords: *Pedro Almodóvar; Pain and Glory; ageing; decline; time; space; death; creativity; remembering; La Movida*

Introduction

Pedro Almodóvar's film *Dolor y gloria* (*Pain and Glory*) (2019) is a physical, mental, and cinematographic journey through time and space. The main character's (Salvador Mallo) journey from childhood to the third age is remembered and (re)created through the memories triggered by heroin. Salvador's memories are filtered by the concept of ageing as decline (Gullette 2004), illness, and death that is first manifested in the figure of his mother, and subsequently in himself. By describing his passage from midlife (crisis) to the third age as the accumulation of ailments and lack of sexual desire, Salvador follows the medicalisation of old age and conceptualises it as the final decline towards death. Through heroin and cinema, he is not only able to get rid of the pain but also to 'move back' to his own 'happy' past in a clear idealisation of childhood (as well as of the mother) in contrast to late life.

This chapter aims to analyse *Pain and Glory* as a metaphorical and creative journey of the ageing self. On the one hand, this journey is shaped by the concept of ageing as illness and decline and by the nostalgic act of confronting death through remembering and recreating an irrecoverable past. For instance, it is this almost universalised concept of ageing as decline (Gullette 2004) that allows global audiences to effortlessly identify with Salvador's experience. On the other hand, this analysis addresses how Almodóvar uses internal migration flows in Spain during the 50s and 60s to depict and idealise a lost past. For example, whereas his childhood in the poor rural Spain of the early fifties is romanticised by using an array of well-known stereotypes about Spain that are easily understood by global audiences, Salvador's move to Madrid in the 80s (the less globally known part of Almodóvar's career) is not directly presented on screen. His life there is recalled through two male figures close to him who reappear in the present: Alberto (the star of his early film *Sabor*) and Federico (Salvador's lover). Madrid in the 80s is indirectly depicted as the centre of creativity and homosexuality, but also as the space in which drugs killed and destroyed the lives of many. It is a city from which Salvador is able to escape thanks to the global success of his films, but a city to which he consistently returns. Therefore, Madrid in the 21st century is portrayed as the space in which Salvador's physical 'decline' and his creative 'resurrection' can coexist. This chapter also explores how late-life creativity (both within and outside of the film) is conceived as a time for recycling memories, and the film itself as the space for recycling Salvador's earlier films to show his global glory.

The film *Pain and Glory* follows the life of a film director, Salvador Mallo (Antonio Banderas), through three narrative storylines. In the first storyline, we see his present life – a depressed filmmaker in his 60s who has been diagnosed with Forestier's Syndrome.[1] After having achieved big successes, he now lives a lonely life marked by illness and a lack of creative inspiration. A second storyline shares young Salvador's loving relationship with his mother Jacinta (Penélope Cruz). In between these two narrative threads, the film offers a third one, a middle-aged man looking after his mother before she dies. By using prolepsis and analepsis, the narrative oscillates between the three timelines to show us snippets of Salvador's life across the years. However, as the audience will realise at the end of the film, which one of these three times is real and not fictional is not an easy question to answer.

Spatially, these three storylines are set in two places: the rural and poor Paterna (childhood) and the urban and rich city of Madrid (from the 80s – the Movida – to the present time). In between these two spaces, Salvador travels around the world as an acclaimed and award-winning film director. But again, the end of the film has the function of blurring the boundaries between real spaces and staged ones, thus problematising any possible connection between the film's events and Almodóvar's real life.

Some scholars have divided Almodóvar's films into two periods: a first one characterised by comedy and domestic tones in which the reversal of gender roles is foregrounded (Poyato 2015; Martínez Cano 2020) and a second one characterised by the dramatic tones that emerge from

---

1   Diffuse idiopathic skeletal hyperostosis (DISH) is a condition commonly affecting male individuals older than 50 years of age. It is characterized by calcification (bony hardening) of ligaments, tendons, and joint capsule insertions (Mader, Verlaan and Buskila 2013, 741).

the centrality that desire, pain, loss, and death acquire (Poyato 2015, 9). Paul Julian Smith (2003) denominates these two periods (following Picasso's creative stages) the *pink period* – films until 1995—and the *blue period* –films from 1995 onwards). Smith describes the gayness that characterises the pink period disappears in the blue period. Barbara Zecchi (2015), following Smith's division, argues that these two periods highlight the evolution of Almodóvar's cinema from optic to haptic, or as she claims, from gay to new queer. Rooting both periods in the transgression of the heteronormative hegemonic gaze, Zecchi (2015) notes that the second period moves beyond the festive transgression of the optic period towards a haptic period that stresses the destabilisation of sexual identity.

Josep M. Armengol and Agustina Varela-Manograsso (2022) have approached *Pain and Glory* from the perspectives of ageing studies, queer studies, and sociology. They argue that the film articulates the idea that gay men are frightened of ageing due to the celebration of youth that the gay culture has focused on. Moreover, they highlight that the "youthism" of gayness has stereotyped older gays as "dirty old men", which clearly results in the scarcity of positive cultural images of older gay men. Another important point that these scholars raise is the possibility of approaching this Almodóvar's film from Jack Halberstam's (2005) notion of "queer time", thus challenging chrononormativity. Recently, Heather Jeronimo (forthcoming 2023) has tackled the film from the intersection of ageing, queer, and disability studies and rightly claims that the film *Pain and Glory* not only reveals the anxieties about old age but also misses the opportunity of locating ageing outside the binary of successful ageing/ageing as decline and making it queer.

Smith (2021) suggests that the film has three main themes: autobiography or autofiction; fluidity or liquidity; and creativity and sexuality. He claims that the initial autobiographical tone set by Banderas in the first sequences soon gives way to autofiction, in which the referent is not his life but his own films. With regards to fluidity and liquidity, Smith stresses the recurrence of water in the film (swimming pool, river, etc.) and associates it with an eroticism that transcends linearity through its persistence in time and space and therefore renders past and present as simultaneous. Finally, Smith points out that Salvador's loss of sexual drive is parallel to his loss of creativity, which clearly differs from his youthful, happy, and sexually transgressive years of La Movida.

Some scholars have traced the autobiographical quality of the film, and therefore have stressed the parallelisms found between Almodóvar's life and the stories and characters presented in the film (Martínez Expósito 2021). The consensus seems to be that Almodóvar's film is autofiction or a fictional autobiography (Smith 2021; Martínez Expósito 2021; Gómez Gómez 2021); but one that intends to blur the autobiographical aspects and moments through different narrative techniques such as fragmentation of important life episodes and intertextuality. Martínez Expósito highlights that the fragmentation and rearrangement of the episodes is one of the distancing devices that Almodóvar uses most frequently in his films (2021, 86). Distancing the viewer from the events allows the filmmaker to make the viewer experience fragmentation as well as the need to actively participate in the chronological rearrangement of fragments.

The film is constructed through three parallel stories: the present time of the depressed and ill Salvador Mallo, his childhood, and his years as a filmmaker during the 1980s. The past, then, is inserted into the present through either flashbacks that the viewer believes to have been triggered by drugs or by the performance of the monologue *Adicción* (Addiction) that Salvador has written. From a psychoanalytical perspective, Shaila García Catalán and Aarón Rodríguez Serrano (2021) consider that *Pain and Glory* underlines the importance of the first desire that occurs in childhood. They claim that the film shows that the emptiness and pain experienced in the present by the body is overcome by artistic sublimation, which involves knowing how to give form to formless pain. After all, there is no glory without pain. That is, a work of art – in this case a film – can be a creation through which the author manages to inhabit the world: art as salvation (Rodríguez Serrano 2021, 98). For instance, Deleuze's analysis of Proust's *In Search of Lost Time* shows that the novel is not simply about time or memory but about apprenticeship, which is one of the revelations of art (*Deleuze* 2000 [1970]). The same can be said about *Pain and Glory*, where the first homoerotic desire is aesthetically embellished and sublimated to make it artistically appear as important in the present as it was in the past. Nonetheless, the first desire can now only be artistically reproduced, thus highlighting that it has been lost.

The film *Pain and Glory* is in fact a nostalgic trip to the childhood of a gay man whose ageing is presented as mental and physical decline. This nostalgic return – induced by drugs – allows Salvador Mallo, the filmmaker, to regain his creativity and thus find refuge from ageing and death in the desire felt for his own art. Furthermore, the two periods in Almodóvar's film pointed out by Smith (2021) and Zecchi (2015) become the subject and form of the film by, on the one hand, presenting the absence of the festive and transgressive gay gaze; and, on the other hand, by focusing on touching (Zecchi 2015) and on sound, while privileging a static gaze by offering long-duration shots in which movement is absent and therefore resembles a painting. In fact, it can be argued that the film *Pain and Glory* is constructed as a series of fragments that reinforce the lack of the most important feature of cinema, movement, while (re)creating an imaginary past in which what is supposed to be absent in the present is present there. However, this statism and this absence would foreground Deleuze's claim that it is the present (and the future), and not the past that is important: "We write not with childhood memories but through blocs of childhood that are the becoming-child of the present" (Deleuze and Guattari 1994, 168).

Ageing: Time and Space

Already in 2016, Almodóvar expressed in a press conference at the Cannes Film Festival that he shared Phillip Roth's notion that "old age is not an illness but a massacre" (Yáñez 2016). This negative concept of ageing clearly offers a socially conformed idea of ageing as a string of ailments and pains, and consequently the medicalisation of ageing – visits to doctors, medication, and surgery – has an important role in the experience of the third and fourth ages. Ageing, then, is seen as the path to death through a biological lens that is filled with losses. Dying, the end of existence, is the ultimate massacre of ageing.

The first consequence of this medicalisation of old age is the notion that 'any time in the past was better' than the present. The second one is that the medicalisation of old age (and the proximity of death) brings a nostalgic return to the place of his childhood, a return that is triggered by Salvador's melancholic state in the present – a state of deep sadness. However, this nostalgic journey to childhood that the film undertakes is determined by the nostalgic wish for childhood and youth themselves (Grassi and De Vita 2016). In this sense, the recollection of his childhood in Paterna is highly idealised around the figure of the mother, the brightness of sunny Paterna, the whiteness/purity of the cave houses and the experience of the first time of sexual desire.

Ageing in *Pain and Glory* is conceived in its linearity and as the pathway to death. The binary of youth versus old age is synonym to others such as active versus passive or productive versus unproductive. Therefore, even if it is only at the level of fiction, Almodóvar in this film, as I argue in the lines that follow, purposefully seeks to deconstruct time and space in order to overcome the chronicity of heteronormative time, the passing of time, the ageing process, and the unavoidable presence of death.

Jan Baars (2013), using Paul Ricoeur's concept of time, has point out that "human aging is basically living (in) time" (143) and "time slips away because we are living (in) it" (2013, 144). Chronological time has been used to measure human ageing with a beginning – birth – and an end – death – and therefore chronometric time relays on a calendar to count days, weeks, months, and years (Baars 2013, 146–147). Despite chronometric age being employed by institutions to regulate labour processes such as retirement, it does not say anything about either individual or collective peculiarities of ageing because ageing depends on biological, economic, social, racial, ethnic, gender and cultural attributes (Cruikshank 2013; Gullette 2004).

In addition to chronological time, narrativity has also been approached in its linearity. For instance, in "Narrative Time" (1980), Paul Ricoeur urged to escape the dichotomy between the chronology of sequence and the a-chronology of models (169). He also pointed out that narrativity and temporality are reciprocal: "Indeed, I take temporality to be that structure of existence that reaches language in narrativity and narrativity to be the language structure that has temporality as its ultimate referent" (Ricoeur 1980, 169). As an intrinsic feature of narrative, the narrative is a subjective representation of a story that can be recounted in a non-linear manner. This absence of linearity results in experiencing time in an achronological way and using memory to manipulate time. For instance, Salvador's account of his life is deployed through three narrative vehicles that problematise time linearity at the narrative level of both the film itself and in Salvador's life. These three levels are the heroin-triggered memories about his childhood in the present time, his non-drug induced memories of his middle-aged years, and the memories inscribed and narrated in the film he is finally making.

The regulatory quality of heteronormative time established by institutions characterises time by its productivity at both the workforce level and in the family space. Elizabeth Freeman (2019) explains that subjectivity is a matter of timing, a normative behaviour that allows us to master time through chrononormativity: the organisation of individuals toward maximum productivity. In addition, Halberstam (2005) has located childhood as the time in which "the conventional logics of development, maturity, adulthood and responsibility" (13) can be disturbed and therefore could offer a more fluid notion of time and gender. Childhood then, as explored by Kerry H. Robinson (2012), can be approached as a queer time and space that deploys alternative imaginings of childhood and different performances of gender. Furthermore, these alternative imaginings of childhood strongly contrast with the regulatory heteronormativity that the institutions of Catholicism, education, and the family, imposed on the child to make sure that there is a 'normal' transition from childhood to adulthood.

According to García Catalán and Rodríguez Serrano (2021), and which is of crucial importance, the structure of the film responds to the temporality of desire; a temporality that always belongs to the past and therefore can only be remembered and re-written/filmed through what they called the eroticism of time (100). Almodóvar's film relies on the first desire to narrate Salvador's autobiography. Salvador's present ailments and pains, along with the reality of ageing, place the film director not only in a melancholic state but also in a chronicity that presents him with a dark future, that of death. The fear of ageing and death makes him travel to the past through memory and through an artistic recreation that constantly underlines the first homoerotic desire felt by Salvador when he was a child. To do so, the recreation takes place through the representation of happiness and pleasure linked, as explained later, to water, music, colour, light, writing and art.

The life of young Salvador in Paterna is surrounded by the figure of the mother and the presence of Eduardo, the mason painter. Two figures that underscore the absence of the most important institutions in his innocent childhood: family, Catholicism, and education. On the one hand, the character of the father disappears from the film as soon as the family of three moves to Paterna; and, on the other hand, Salvador has self-taught himself to write and read and will teach Eduardo. It is not until the visit of Beata – an authoritative figure dressed in black (Susi Sánchez) – that the institutions of Catholicism and education are introduced, and the life of Salvador takes a radical turn. Immediately linking *Pain and Glory* to Almodóvar's 2004 film *La mala educación (The Bad Education)*, the boy is awarded a scholarship to attend a strict Catholic boarding school in which his voice soon attracts the attention of the priest who serves as a singing teacher. The intertextuality with *La mala educación*, as well as the swims the young boys take in the river, make the audience aware of the Catholic Church's sexual abuses that Spanish children endured during (and after) Franco's regime. This is the moment in which Salvador's innocence is lost, prompting him to initiate the passage from childhood to adulthood; a passage that brings an important change in the notion of time: from a queer time – porous and fluid – to a rigid (hetero)normative time.

The first sequences show mother and son by the river years before moving to Paterna. The next time we see mother and son together, they are in a train station[2] in which they must spend the night before they arrive in Paterna, a town where his father has been working with the hope of leaving poverty behind. The Spanish Civil War and the colossal poverty that Spain had to endure during the first few decades of Franco's dictatorship had a huge impact on agriculture which would lead eventually to a massive exodus from the rural areas during the 1940s, which continued throughout the 1950s and 1960s. Internal migration flows from rural areas to areas in which the industry was prominent were quite frequent and massive during those decades. Paterna, a town five kilometres away from Valencia, in the 50s benefited from the construction of an industrial area thus attracting a high number of workers. At the beginning of the 20th Century, 40% of the town's population lived in caves, but in the 50s, they started to be abandoned by their inhabitants (Ayuntamiento de Paterna n.d.). The audience can assume then that Salvador's father gets one of those abandoned caves because of the poverty of the family. The dark cave is artistically turned into a lively and warm home by the mother Jacinta and the young illiterate and handsome mason painter Eduardo. However, only Salvador's eyes capture the idyllic quality of life in Paterna. In fact, Jacinta, although she clearly tries to make a home in the cave, does not hide her dislike of the place and her desire to spare Salvador a life of hardships. The impossibility of the poor to have an education impels Jacinta to send Salvador to the seminary but what the child encounters is poor education and a high level of sexual abuse at the hands of the priests.

Life before and in Paterna is therefore highly idealised by using bright colours, the radiance of the sun, the whiteness of the cave, and the beautiful singing of the women washing clothes in the river. Salvador's homosexual desire is awakened by seeing the mason painter washing himself after working on painting the cave and the light touch of their hands when he teaches Eduardo to read and write. Hence reality is presented to the viewer through Salvador's innocent young eyes, thus not showing either his family's poverty or that of those around him. In addition, men who are part of his childhood and puberty are

---

2   The viewer will learn at the end of the film that the train station is a filming set.

either connected to his soon-to-flourish homosexual desire (the mason painter), sexual abuse (the Catholic priests), or the absent figure of the father. By contrast, the present life of Salvador in Madrid, as well as his life looking after his mother in Madrid, are presented mainly in modern but enclosed spaces in which, despite the presence of bright colours, darkness and artificiality seem to be predominant. The river is transformed into a swimming pool; the sketch painting on cardboard by the mason painter is replaced by expensive paintings hanging on the walls by well-known artists such as Maruja Mallo – from whom Almodóvar borrows Salvador's surname – Guillermo Pérez Villalta, Sigfrido Martín Begué, and Manolo Quejido, among others. The idealised and gentle mother of his childhood is at the present of the narration dead but is the protagonist of one of the stories told in achronological order. She is in fact depicted when she is ill and aged, thus emphasising her loss and decline. This depiction of loss, in addition, is accompanied by a characterisation of the mother in the present as not gentle as the one from childhood, one that is sometimes cruel and unempathetic.[3] Salvador anticipates himself the physical and emotional deterioration of his mother, thus driving him to an antithetical emotional response to his own mother: his love for her and his rejection of her as an incarnation of ageing and death. Therefore, loss impregnates his relationship with his mother as well as his present condition as an ageing person.

Aging as Loss: Time, Space, and Identity

A life review such as the one undertaken by Almodóvar allows the ageing person not only to rememorate their own life but also to reflect on what has been lost and what has remained. In other words, the perception of ageing as loss and decline permits Mallo/Almodóvar to see both ageing and death as the greatest threat to his sense of self and therefore seeks

---

3   Mothers and motherhood are recurrent topics in his films. From good to bad mothers, from tyrannical mothers to servile ones.

to remain in time through the recreation of his early cinematographic pieces as a way to beat death and loss.

Salvador's perspective of loss seems to emanate from everything in his life: loss of youth, loss of physical and mental abilities, loss of health, loss of sexual drive, loss of his mother, loss of social activities, loss of creativity, and his own death as the ultimate loss. His identity as an internationally acclaimed filmmaker is accompanied, according to Salvador's chronological narrative, by the understanding and learning of the numerous ailments that after the age of thirty affected, and still affect, his body and his mind: insomnia, gastric reflux and ulcers, asthma, sciatica, all kind of muscular pains, tinnitus, sibilancies, migraines, tension headaches, back pain and back surgery, panic attacks, depression, and anxiety. Body and mental health problems define his present life and result in his loneliness and lack of creativity. The return to childhood is then triggered by the film director's need to escape his present state of pain and suffering, as well as the unavoidable closeness to death.[4]

Qingyang Zhou (2020) has pointed out that the nostalgic remembering of Salvador's childhood foregrounds an unrealistic pastoral portrayal of post-Civil War rural Spain. In this sense, and following Sara Amhed's ideas, Zhou suggests that Salvador is in fact overcoming his drug addiction and creativity impasse through the creation of a "fetishized place of no return" (Zhou 2020, n.p.) and Almodóvar's metafictional insertion of the film within a film proposes "the role of cinema to record, realize, and eternalize Salvador's memories of home and homosexuality." (Zhou 2020, n.p.) That is, Zhou (2020) considers this idealisation of childhood, and its filmic recreation, to be like those narratives of migration and estrangement examined by Ahmed and her notion of identity as movement and loss. Ahmed (1999) explains that,

> Migration involves not only a spatial dislocation, but also a temporal dislocation: 'the past' becomes associated with a home that it is

---

4   Interestingly, Banderas' body – despite his heart attack at the age of 56 – is quite fit and does not really match the body of someone who is suffering from so many ailments and does not exercise.

impossible to inhabit, and be inhabited by, in the present. The question then of being at home or leaving home is always a question of memory, of the discontinuity between past and present (343).

It is therefore important to stress that ageing in its chronicity is in fact a temporal movement that accentuates loss and the discontinuity, as expressed by Ahmed, of past and present. It is precisely, as she claims, memory that emphasises discontinuity and dislocation, and generates the fragmented narrative of *Pain and Glory*. In this sense, it is important to note that all parts of Salvador Mallo's/Pedro Almodóvar's story/life are only told through texts: childhood through film; the years of La Movida through a staged monologue; the years of success through an infographic, etc. By not 'showing' a whole period of the past on the screen – early adulthood –, only 'telling' about it and only 'showing' the characters in their current state in the present – a filmmaker who cannot create due to his mental and physical ailments; an actor who cannot perform due to his addictions; and a former gay lover who has now married a woman and is a father – the film reinforces the idea of ageing as decline. This idea of decline is even more evident in the relationship with the mother: the idealisation of the mother in Salvador's nostalgic return to childhood and the reality of an older – and at some points monstrous mother – that makes Salvador face the unavoidable reality of death and dying. Furthermore, by omitting 'showing' adulthood, the film deconstructs the linearity of time: Although chronological time exists, it can be altered and manipulated within the artistic representation.

Another way to blur the chronological narrative is, as mentioned before, the use of fictional narratives within the film to evoke and depict memories. Consequently, this use of diverse fictional narratives puts into question the veracity of those memories and their rendering. Almodóvar's relentless use of his previous films as intertexts functions as a way of self-referentiality at both creative and personal levels and emphasises the imaginative and creative nature of memory. Marsha Kinder (2009) analyses Almodóvar's intertextuality as a kind of "retroseriality" that stresses not only an aspect of his filmmaking but also one that leads the viewer on how to understand the film (269). Indeed, this same technique emerges in *Pain and Glory* referring to (and I would add *honouring*) his previous films.

Furthermore, the final sequence acquires special meaning within this context of the metafictional structure by stressing the story of Salvador's childhood we have been watching as part of older Salvador's return to his past through memory is Salvador's film. The train station in which mother and son must sleep before being able to get to Paterna is a film set. Confronted with this ending, the viewer realises that the future (filming a new movie) is no longer the future, thus breaking again with chronologic time. But the viewer also comprehends that a new layer of artistic work has been added to the structure of the film, hence emphasising memory as a construction, and underlying the aesthetic construction of reality. It can be argued that Pedro Almodóvar superimposes two thematic areas: that of the history of the person Salvador Mallo and that of the creator Salvador Mallo, thus prompting the viewer to actively participate in the film by either having to chronologically reorder the story or by rejecting to reorder the story, hence accepting a new non-heteronormative time.

The closing sequence of the film impels the viewer to understand Salvador's childhood in Paterna like the fictional narrative that Salvador Mallo, the film director, is writing and then filming. The discovery of Salvador's portrait and the inscription on it prompts Salvador to write *The First Desire* (not his love relationship with Federico or Marcelo in *Addiction*), which in fact will be the script of the film he will shoot and will be used to frame the story of transformation from pain to glory of the older Salvador. Furthermore, recreating a first desire that was never fulfilled adds another layer of idealisation that the "love of his life", Federico, lacks due to his heroin addiction. Memories are recalled with nostalgic tones, written and cinematically recreated. The ending sequence is in fact the beginning of a new stage in Salvador's identity that projects himself to a future of gain and not loss; an identity that finally does not have to nostalgically remember the past because he is making it eternally present through film. The cinematic recreation of his life is in fact a way to endlessly (re)live it and consequently transform loss into gain and glory. Cinema becomes a space in which to create a fresh identity for Salvador, thus displacing ageing by generating this timeless eternity.

However, if his childhood is a film, his youth and the years as the icon of La Movida are a play, hence producing a further personal detachment from his personal/real identity and highlighting his identity as an acclaimed author/filmmaker/playwright. Salvador gives Alberto his confessional monologue *Adicción* to be performed and signed by the latter as a way to tell Salvador's life in the 1980s without being recognised by the public neither as the protagonist of the story nor its author. Hiding his identity and story behind fictional names and a fake author and performer, the monologue stresses its performative quality and hence allows the main character to emotionally detach from it once it has been written. Nevertheless, the love of his life in the 80s – Federico in the film and Marcelo in the play—is attending the play and recognises the melodramatic love story that *Adicción* narrates. This identification results in emotionally approaching the viewer of *Pain and Glory* to Salvador's story – the viewers and Alberto are the only ones aware of the real authorship of the confessional monologue. But ultimately, this identification with Salvador as the author of the story places the viewer simultaneously inside and outside the film when cinema is again central: "El amor tal vez mueva montañas, pero no basta para salvar a la persona que quieres ... Yo me quedé en Madrid y el cine me salvó." (Love may move mountains, but it is not enough to save the person you love ... I stayed in Madrid and the cinema saved me) (*Pain and Glory*). Now the viewer not only links the monologue to Salvador Mallo but also to Pedro Almodóvar.

Conclusion

The seventeen-century Spanish writer Pedro Calderón de la Barca had claimed in his 1636 masterpiece *La vida es sueño* (*Life Is a Dream*) that life is an illusion, a dream; that is, the only reality is to be found in the invisible and eternal. Leaving aside the philosophical overtones of Calderón's piece, *Pain and Glory* seems to be adapting the idea of the dreams to the idea that life is cinema and cinema is just cinema.[5] This idea is reiterated in several ways throughout the film: through songs, films, paintings, etc. With regards to songs, Almodóvar employs the 1961 song *Come Sinfonia* (*Like a Symphony*) by the Italian singer Mina. This song talks about how through dreams one can get closer to the person one loves and cannot be with: "Sogno... Sogno... (I dream... I dream...) / e tu sei con me (and you are with me) / ... / io vorrei, io vorrei (I would like, I would like)/ che questo sogno fosse realtà (That this dream was a reality) / Realtà d'un sogno d' amor (reality of a love dream)." Another technique used is the recurrent use of elements in the film that somehow resemble a film screen: the whiteness of sheets left to air dry, the whiteness of the cave's walls and the film screen behind Alberto's monologue in *Adicción*. In the monologue, Mallo as an author explains how in his childhood movies were played on white walls. He goes on telling the films he remembers the most: films with water. While Alberto plays this part, he evokes the waterfalls, beaches, rivers, and springs that he remembers from the films watched, and these are projected on a portable screen situated behind Alberto. These scenes of water are, in addition, accompanied by shots of big stars such as Warren Beatty and Natalie Wood in Elia Kazan's *Splendor in the Grass* (1961) and Marylin Monroe. Moreover, Anna Magnani in *Mamma Roma* (1962), by Pier Paolo Pasolini, and Sofía Loren are two of the actresses that inform both the acting of Penélope Cruz and the cinematography of José Luis Alcaide, thus making cinema even more central in terms of form and content.

All these intertexts and references to an auto-fictional past which dates back to the 1960s explain not only Mallo's imagery but Almodóvar's as well. The constant intertextuality stresses not only the artificiality of cinema, but also its agelessness. Cinema, as the artefact it is, is eternal while life is time passing; therefore, the question would be whether the art/ifice of Mallo's new film not only recreates the past, or makes it present again, but if his art becomes ageless. Otto Rank (1983), Hannah

---

5   The twentieth-century Spanish singer and songwriter Luis Eduardo Aute would sing in 1984: "More cinema please / that everything in life is cinema / that everything in life is cinema / and dreams cinema is."

Arendt (2013 [1958]), and Zygmunt Bauman (1998) have all discussed the links established between death and immortality by modernity. Bauman (1998) argues that the history of art is a continuous effort to go beyond the brief time of biological life; a frantic effort to eradicate the most inhuman consequences of man's mortality. However, he also acknowledges that postmodernity rejects durability and stability to favour change and flexibility and therefore postmodern men's and women's lives are organised around desires desiring to desire. That is, the eternal time is decomposed in postmodernity into a succession of fragmented episodes that are valued and justified in terms of their capacity to provide momentary satisfaction. It can be argued, going back to Halberstam's notion of the fluidity of time in childhood and the changes expressed by the notion of art between modernity and postmodernity, that *Pain and Glory* emerges as a film in which ageing as an expression of death gives voice to the struggle between the timelessness of art, the immortality of the artist, and the notion of fluid time.

Almodóvar's incessant framing and reframing of his own work and the work of others, his appropriation of the work of others through intertextuality or acting, proves that his notion of art contains the notions of art above mentioned: change, fragmentation, and recyclability allow art to be eternal thanks to being recycled. Almodóvar not only appropriates the work of Kazan, for example, when including him in his own films, but also positions himself at the same level as his predecessors and as part of the history of filmmaking. Consequently, his films are his identity; his cinematography is not only his home but also his path to immortality and glory. Pain is what makes us temporal, glory atemporal.

References

Ahmed, Sara. "Home and away: Narratives of migration and estrangement." *International Journal of Cultural Studies* 2(3) (1999): 329–347. https://doi.org/10.1177/136787799900200303.

Arendt, Hannah. *The human condition*. Chicago: University of Chicago Press, 2013.

Armengol, Josep M. and Agustina Varela-Monograsso. "*Pain and Glory*: Narrative (De)Constructions of Older Gay Men in Contemporary Spanish Culture and Cinema." *Journal of Aging Studies*, 63 (2022): 1–9. https://doi.org/10.1016/j.jaging.2022.101030.

Aute, Luis Eduardo. "Más cine, por favor". *Cuerpo a cuerpo*. Ariola Records, 1984.

Ayuntamiento de Paterna. "Paterna." http://www.paterna.es:88/web/ve r_pagina.asp?id=159.

Baars, Jan. "Critical Turns of Aging, Narrative and Time." *International Journal of Aging and Later Life* 7.2 (2012): 143–165.

Bauman, Zygmunt. "On Art, Death and Postmodernity – And What They Do to Each Other".*Stopping the Process: Contemporary View on Art and Exhibition*. Ed. M. Hannula. Helsinki: Nordic Institute for Contemporary Art, (1998). 21–34.

Calderón de la Barca, P. *Life Is a Dream*. Trans. E. Fitzgerald. (2006). http s://www.gutenberg.org/files/2587/2587-h/2587-h.htm.

Cruikshank, Margaret. *Learning to be old: Gender, culture, and aging*. Rowman & Littlefield Publishers, 2013.

Deleuze, Gilles and Félix Guattari. *What is Philosophy?* Trans. H. Tomlinson and G. Burchell III. New York: Columbia University Press, 1994.

Deleuze, Gilles. *Proust and Signs: The Complete Text*. Minnesota: University of Minnesota Press, 2000.

Dolor y Gloria (Pain and Glory). Directed by Pedro Almodóvar, El Deseo, 2019.

Freeman, Elizabeth. "The Queer Temporalities of Queer Temporalities." GLQ: A Journal of Lesbian and Gay Studies 25.1 (2019): 91–95. García Catalán, Shaila and Aarón Rodríguez Serrano. "La pantalla fetiche: deseo y sublimación en *Dolor y gloria* de Pedro Almodóvar." *Journal of Spanish Cultural Studies* 22.1, (2021): 95–110.

Gómez Gómez, Agustín. "'Dolor y gloria', ¿autobiografía, autoficción o ficción autobiográfica audiovisual?" *Pasavento* IX.2, (2021): 405–423.

Grassi, Ludovica, and Clelia De Vita. "Nostalgia between mourning and melancholia." *L'Autre* 17.3 (2016): 321–329.

Gullette, Margaret Morganroth. *Aged by culture*. Chicago: University of Chicago Press, 2004.

Halberstam, Jack. *In a Queer Time and Place: Transgender Bodies, Subcultural Lives*. New York and London: New York University Press, 2005.

Jeronimo, Heather. "Masculinity, Creativity, and Successful Ageing in Pedro Almodóvar's *Pain and Glory* (2019)". *Ageing Masculinities in Contemporary European and Anglophone Cinema*. Eds. Tony Tracy and Michaela Schrage-Früh. London: Routledge, forthcoming 2023.

Kinder, Marsha. "All About the Brothers: Retroseriality in Almodóvar's Cinema." *All About Almodóvar: A Passion for Cinema*, Eds. Brad Epps & Despina Kakoudaki. Minnesota: Monnesota UP, 2009. 267–294.*La mala educación (The Bad Education)*. Directed by Pedro Almodóvar, El Deseo, 2004.

Mader, Reuven, Verlaan, Jorrit Jean, & Buskila, Dan. "Diffuse idiopathic skeletal hyperostosis: clinical features and pathogenic mechanisms." *Nature reviews. Rheumatology* 9.12, (2013): 741–750.

Mamma Roma. Directed by Pier Paolo Pasolini, Arco Film Roma, 1962.

Martínez Expósito, Alfredo. "La escena primordial en "Dolor y gloria" de Pedro Almodóvar." *Estudios Hispánicos* XXIX (2021): 85–93. https://doi.org/10.19195/2084-2546.29.9.

Martínez-Cano, Francisco Javier. "El cine como tecnología de género. Transgresiones formales en la construcción de la identidad sexual en el cine de Almodóvar". *Construcciones culturales y políticas del género*. Eds. Eva Hernández Martínez, José Manuel López-Agulló Pérez Caballero & Sergio Marín Conejo. Sevilla: Dykinson, 2020.

Mina. "Come Sinfonia", Italdisc, Italy, 1961.

Poyato Sánchez, Pedro *Identidad visual y forma narrativa en el drama cinematográfico de Almodóvar*. Madrid: Editorial Síntesis, 2015.

Rank, Otto. "Life and Creation." *Literature and Psychoanalysis*. Columbia: Columbia University Press, 1983. 39–54.

Ricoeur, Paul. "Narrative Time." *Critical Inquiry* 7.1 (1980): 169–190.

Robinson, Kerry H. "Childhood as A 'Queer Time and Space': Alternative Imaginings of Normative Markers of Gendered Lives." *Queer and Subjugated Knowledge*. Eds. Bronwyn Davies, Kerry H. Robinson and Cristyn Davies, 2012. 110–139.

Smith, Paul Julian. "Pasión y redención: el envejecimiento en Almodóvar." *Envejecimiento y cines ibéricos*. Eds. Barbara Zecchi, Raquel Medina, Cristina Moreiras, Pilar Rodríguez. Valencia: Tirant lo Blanc, 2021: 79–93.

Smith, Paul Julian. *Contemporary Spanish Culture. TV, Fashion, Art and Film*. Malden: Blackwell, 2003.

Splendor in the Grass. Directed by Elia Kazan, Elia Kazan production, 1961.

Yáñez, Manu. "Almodóvar: "Si los papeles de panamá fueran una película, nosotros seríamos unos extras." 2016. https://www.fotogramas.es/festival-de-cannes/a15115755/almodovar-si-los-papeles-de-panama-fueran-una-pelicula-nosotros-seriamos-unos-extras/

Zecchi, Barbara. "El cine de Pedro Almodóvar: De óptico a háptico, De gay a 'new queer'". *Área Abierta* 15.1 (2015): 31–52.

Zhou, Qingyang. "Negotiating the Concept of National Allegory: Homosexuality, Departure, and Homecoming in Pedro Almodóvar's Pain and Glory and Midi Z's Nina Wu." *Inquiries Journal* 12.09 (2020). http://www.inquiriesjournal.com/a?id=1789

The Celluloid Hurdles
Israeli Women Film Directors in the Prism of Gender and Time

Shlomit Aharoni Lir and Liat Ayalon

Abstract: *This qualitative study explores the role of personal and historical time in the power dynamics that women encounter in the Israeli film industry. Based on a close thematic analysis of 26 interviews with women film directors in the film "In the Director's Chair Sits a Woman" (2020), the findings suggest that women in the Israeli film industry continue to face unique obstacles that prolong or block their professional advancement. The study proposes four metaphors that capture specific axes that intersect time, cinema and gender. Firstly, "uncertain time" refers to the loss of precious time that women in cinema experience due to gendered stereotypes about women's ability to direct. Secondly, "the time loop" denotes having to face stereotypical gendered norms and recurrent instances where women directors are forced to reshoot scenes due to male obstinacy on the set. Thirdly, the "sliding doors" metaphor captures how women are forced to choose between two life trajectories, focused either on childbearing or on filmmaking. Lastly, "time standing still" addresses setbacks related to women's experiences of sexual harassment and sexual assault as part of their work in the film industry. In addition, we chose the metaphor "gendered historical time" to indicate the significant change that is gradually taking place in the film industry, in everything related to gender equality.*

Keywords: *Israeli women in cinema; women and time; gender equality; celluloid ceiling; power relations; feminism*

Introduction

The metaphor of the "glass ceiling", first coined in the 1970s, does not directly relate to the aspect of lost time in women's careers. Instead, it calls attention to the invisible barriers that lead to the increasingly homogenous masculine gender dominance that emerges the higher up the professional ladder one climbs (Cotter, Hermsen, Ovadia and Vanneman 2001). However, the notion of lost time is inferred by the metaphor, when thinking of the efforts many women face trying to break the various concealed ceilings they confront in their professional life. Following this conceptualization, more than twenty years later, the "celluloid ceiling" metaphor was repurposed for indicating the unseen barriers that stand in the way of women in the film industry (Lauzen 2011). Again, the aspect of lost time can only be induced from reading the annual reports of the Center for the Study of Women in Television and Film which began recording women's status in the film industry in the United States in 1998. Similarly, when Israel had joined what had quickly become an international effort, and issued a report that provided concentrated numerical data recording the heavily gendered state of affairs in the local television and film industries, women's loss of time was not a central issue (Elefant et al. 2021). It could only be inferred from reading the numbers.

The issue of loss of time was not at the center of the worldwide qualitative attempts to understand the underrepresentation of women in the film industry and to explain the gender bias in directorial positions. Yet, the topic of time could often be found in interviews with women directors who produced in-depth accounts of their work behind the camera (Lyden 2018). These endeavors simultaneously document the significant advances that women in the industry have made during the last few decades as well as the many structural time-consuming barriers they continue to grapple with.

In this qualitative study, we focus on the role of time in the professional career of Israeli women film directors. Based on fully transcribed interviews with 26 feature-film directors, who speak directly to the camera about their experiences in the documentary *In the Director's Chair Sits a Woman* (Zamir 2020), we address the question of the role of personal and historical time in the power relations women encounter in the Israeli film industry.

The Marginalization of Women's Voices in Israeli Society and Cinema

Despite its ethos of equality, the social structures that emerged during the early development stages of secular Zionist society deprived women of participating in social life on an equal footing with men (Benjamin 2012; Pfefferman 2011). The marginalization and silencing of women, side by side with the privileged, hegemonic positioning of Israeli men is still evident in Israel today, in the overwhelmingly male-majority representation of professionals working in key state institutions and in political spaces (Tzameret et al. 2021).

This gender-based structural imbalance is reflected in the Israeli film industry, which mirrors and reproduces women's exclusion in a number of ways. Most egregious is the scarcity of women directors: Women directed only 7% of feature films from the establishment of the state until the early 2000s. The gap started to close over the past two decades, but remained distinct as between 2013 and 2018 women directed only 21% of films. Women are also underrepresented in casting, both in the number of roles as well as the scope of roles they play – often supporting roles, whose principal function is to reflect aspects of the male protagonist or protagonists who occupy the center of the plot (Shaer-Meoded 2016; Elefant et al. 2021).

Time and Gender: Between Family and Career

On the surface of things, gender inequality in the film industry is not linked to time. However, while time is a resource that is universal in its uniformity – as we all have the same 24 hours a day – gendered social norms charge one's time with additional meanings. Starting in childhood and increasing in salience in adulthood, social regimes of gender-specific expectations weigh heavily on self-efficacy levels and on professional life patterns. Traditional divisions of labor between women and men accord different social value to ways men and women choose to spend their time. Whereas women are expected to prioritize their familial roles as mothers and housekeepers, men do not face similar expectations when managing their time (Fogel-Bizawi 1999). Studies indicate that despite having entered the labor market in ever increasing numbers in recent decades, on average, women dedicate significantly more time to housekeeping than men. Women thus may have secured the 'right' to work outside the house, but they have overwhelmingly remained the sole parties responsible for managing it (Cerrato and Cifre 2018). Since society expects women to assume responsibility for the caretaking role, the conflict between work and family is a common element in many women's lives. If, in early parenthood, women are considered the principal responsible parties in nursing young children, they are also saddled with the burden of taking care of older people and family members with disability in the later stages of their lives. As a result, women often report a need to find flexible employment, which would permit them to takes prolonged leaves of absence and to resume working in accordance with the fluctuations of their families' needs. Men, by contrast, often assume the role of the principal breadwinner and develop a constant and uninterrupted pattern of participating in the labor market. Hence, it is safe to argue that the conflict between the home and the family is felt particularly strongly and significantly in women's lives (Cerrato and Cifre 2018).

The Present Study

This qualitative research explores the role of time in Israeli women directors' professional life. The study is based on the thematic analysis of 26 interviews with directors documented in the film *In the Director's Chair Sits a Woman* (Zamir 2020). The film, that premiered at the Haifa Film Festival, records the experience of being a woman director in the Israeli film industry that is controlled mainly by men.

As a documentary, the film corresponds with existing literature on gender and filmmaking, setting as its main target to focus on the question of the minority of women directors in the Israeli film industry. This feature turns the film into a unique and valuable source of data. After close examination, which included each of us watching the film twice, and building a table with participants' details, we found that the films is a most suitable source for data analysis, as it provides insights into the worlds of 37% of all women directors of feature films in Israel. The film allowed the directors to narrate their own perspectives on being a woman in the Israeli film industry and to share their personal experiences in their own words, thereby making it especially suitable for qualitative research analysis. Moreover, the fact that the directors interviewed in the film are heterogenous with regard to age, sexual orientation, ethnic origin, and martial situation (e.g., single, married, divorced, with and without children), enabled us to examine commonalities beyond differences in experience. This followed the understanding that the diversity of cases enhances generalization (Ragin and Amoroso 2011).

Method

This research is based on a data corpus that consists of the full transcription of all the interviews in the film. We used thematic analysis in order to identify, analyze, and report patterns within the data (Boyatzis, 1998). Our goal was to capture relevant concepts that were repeated in different interviews.

Our analysis was data-driven; we chose an inductive approach in searching and coding time related themes (Braun and Clarke 2006). We watched the movie a few times and each author read and re-read the transcribed interviews a number of times. We marked topics explicitly related to time where directors talked about time they wasted on their road to filmmaking. We also marked latent and implied notions related to time. Following the process of identifying repeated notions, concepts, and ideas related to time from various interviews, we coded them and divided them into distinct categories (Denzin and Lincoln 1994). The first author took the lead role by developing the preliminary categories related to the concept of time. These categories were subsequently reviewed and elaborated by the second author. Although other topics also emerged in the interviews, such as gender relations or the financial costs associated with producing movies, our focus was exclusively on time. This focus was determined after a thorough reading and re-reading of the transcribed interviews. We analysed our findings from a constructionist perspective, attempting not to focus solely on an individual perspective, but on the socio-cultural and structural basis of various individual accounts (Braun and Clarke 2006).

We acknowledge that the number of interviews was determined by the director. Nonetheless, we have reached thematic saturation even before the 26 interviews were completed as no new data emerged from the text with regard to the concept of time.

Findings

While three directors had explicitly stated that they never felt discriminated against, most of the directors talked about various obstacles limiting their ability to create. Paying close attention to the motif of time, we divided our findings into four categories. The first, "There was no one. Only men", explores the difficulty of being a woman pioneer in a field dominated by men. The second, "A glass ceiling inside your mind", examines experiences of loss of time due to women's socialization. The third, "They had a problem with me calling the shots", portrays difficulties with male crew members and stereotypical thinking that consumes time, as well as a sexist atmosphere that sets women back in the film industry. The fourth, "Did you check the state of your ovaries?", refers to time consuming conflicts between work and motherhood.

"There was no one. Only men."

The few women who were active filmmakers at the onset of Israeli cinema were pioneers of their trade, a fact that carries much significance in terms of the time required to mobilize knowledge and support. Zamir's film begins with revisiting choreographer and director Elida Gera's groundbreaking contribution to cinema, her film *Before tomorrow* (1969), which was the first full-length feature film directed by a woman in Israeli cinematic history. In the archival footage, Gera speaks of her isolation in the field:

> **This wasn't a period of female directors**. In cinema, women were actresses. There might've been an editor or two, and Margot Klausner, who was a big producer. (Elida Gera)[1]

The sense of being a diminutive minority, that women directors born in the early and mid-20th century experienced in their careers, is also described by Dina Zvi-Riklis, who makes a connection between the absence of women in the film industry at large with the time it took her to enter the world of filmmaking:

> **It took me a long, long time** [...] even after having made two short films, I never called myself a director. I looked around me, and only men were directors. Back then, Michal was [...] she did films, Michal Bat-Adam. I think she was the only one. She had experience – she was an actress, too – so she already had a head start. **It was hard, you know, to get into that world** [...] because "director", that's an entire world, it was a huge thing. Monetarily, too, the responsibility [...] of justifying the investment. And there was no support to be had, **you couldn't just phone another director [...] a woman director and tell her: "Listen, I need some tips, how did it go for you? What should I do? Should I insist on that? [...] there was no discussion to be had, because there was no one. Only men.** (Dina Zvi-Riklis)

Zvi-Riklis captures women's experience of time as simultaneously progressing on two axes. On one hand, when there were fewer women filmmakers in cinema, women who succeed in making their way to the director's chair were made to feel self-aware since their professional milieu made them exceptional. This heightened self-awareness made them take longer to develop a distinct professional identity in their field and to

---

1   Emphases, here and elsewhere, are ours.

expend much energy on overcoming self-doubt. On the other hand, this situation also fostered a long-term hope that, the more women would become involved in cinema, the less self-aware women directors would be in the future.

"A glass ceiling inside your mind"

Women are forced to face time wasting obstacles long before they begin their careers, due to societal gendered structures. Actress, screenwriter, playwright, and director Hanna Azoulay-Hasfari recounts her childhood impressions:

> Women are socialized to not want things. Today this had changed, today women do want things. Why is that? It's because they see other women who wanted things, too, and who set out to achieve them [...]. My mother never wanted anything for herself. Which was the worst example I could have been exposed to, as her daughter. This is what women were told [...].
> I never wanted to direct. But the first time I directed, I couldn't, for the life of me, understand why I've never tried it before. When I was a kid, I was student council president, but by the time I got to high-school, all I wanted was for people to fall in love with me. That's all I wanted [...]. It's a striking transition, from a smart girl, a leader, to a girl [...] who diminishes herself, who wanes herself down, because to be loved she obviously can't be a leader, can't be opinionated, can't be this, that, or the other [...]. So I can only imagine that, had I attended a girls-only high-school, for example, I'd cultivate that little leader that I was as a child [...] I'd bring her to a situation where she wants things [...] young woman who stands up for herself, an entrepreneur, a creator, and I would've probably begun directing in my late 20s, not in my late 40s. That's twenty years. Twenty years' hold-up. (Hanna Azoulay Hasfari)

Azoulay Hasfari enhances the understanding of the difficulty of creating without having models of success to look up to or even the reassurance that film directing is a possible and realistic occupation as a woman.

Her description of her transition from an opinionated and smart girl, a leader, to one whose self-esteem depends on being liked is not unique to her, and evokes research on teen-age girls silencing their opinions and desires while seeking attention from teen-age boys (Gilligan 1982).

Career wise, it is possible to conceptualize the process of early loss of the confidence to speak and act out as resulting in loss of precious time. In Azoulay Hasfari's case, it amounts to twenty years' worth of creative work lost. Azoulay Hasfari did eventually attain professional success, won numerous accolades and prizes, and today is rightly considered to be a successful role model. One might suggest that she entered the field with greater insight and life experience. Still, it is worth contemplating what more she could have created had she spent those twenty years busy in professional activity, gaining in-field experience. This question becomes even more poignant when we consider the centrality of experience to refining one's artistic craft and deepening one's authorial voice.

On top of early socialization that discourages women from allowing themselves to dream and invest in their abilities, there are obstacles that stand in the way of women who have the courage to dream but could not pursue their dreams due to social conventions:

> After my grandmother Rivka, peace be upon her, died, I understood that much of that character, the protagonist, of my film "The Mountain", was actually her. And my childhood memories from her, and her pains, that she never left her kitchen [...] there are those women who always say: what good came from feminism? We had it better in the past [...] but **I grew up with a grandmother who always said: "I'm not happy! This isn't what was supposed to happen to me! I was supposed to go out and study chemistry and be like Marie Curie,** not knead Matzah balls in Ramat Gan (Yaelle Kayam)

Kayam's story of her grandmother Rivka's unfulfilled ambitions demonstrates a complete loss of time, where a woman lives without attaining her fullest potential, and all that is left is sorrow.

The aspect of regret over the loss of valuable time due to social constructions that sow self-doubt among women emerged in different interviews in a variety of ways:

> I don't think that the notion that a woman making a film was an obvious and simple thing. Who was I to make a feature? I'd ask. And it took me years to write […] who am I? What am I? […] what will I do? Things that may have been self-evident to others, when they won awards for short films and then went, "Sure, time to do a feature!" and to me it always seemed like "What do you mean? That I oversee a truck and twenty guys and tell them 'go left, go right'? Who am I?" and, say I'd even manage to get the money, what would I do with it? I'd feel like I'm on an expedition to the moon. When Dover (Kosashvili) got money with pre-conditions, he came and told me: '90 days, each day you write one page of text, and voila, you've got yourself a feature […] Me, it took me five years. Everyday I'd wake up and ask "who am I? what am I? me, make a movie? Why ever? […]. I said: 'A million shekels […] all the things one could buy with a million shekels!' […] It's a glass ceiling inside your mind. (Maya Dreifuss)

Past research has located gender differences in diverse expectations of success, showing how women lag behind men in their belief in their ability to succeed as a result of the role of cultural agents, parents, and teachers in forming achievement-related beliefs (Meece, Bower Glienke and Burg 2006). In her early career as a film-director, Dreifuss found it difficult to imagine herself fulfilling the leadership role required of a film director on set. The contrast she draws between Kosashvili who ostensibly writes a script in three months and the five years of self-doubt it took her to write encapsulates the broader story of women struggling alone against social constructs that curtail women's confidence, enabling them to either professionally develop late or not at all.

"They had a problem with me calling the shots"

The social perception and assimilation of gender roles within the film industry form another structural obstacle in the professional careers of women in the field:

> There were some men who [...] hid it, but they didn't do a very good job hiding that they were having a hard time. They had a problem with me calling the shots. With my telling them, "the camera should be here". My insisting, "this high, not that high". With my saying we need a 40mm lens, not 50. They wouldn't admit as much, but it'd be there, in something they did. That [...] suddenly someone'd try, facetiously of course, counteract me [...] here and there, there were some horrible things. I mean, really horrible stuff. (Michal Bat-Adam)

> The first time I wanted to film, I took all the Tel-Avivians to Deir Hanna,[2] to the village. And I had a cameraman who didn't set the camera, and I wanted a fixed shot. And it drove me crazy, that someone altered my decision, and **that he allowed himself to do it, because he thinks he knows better.** And I remember [...] it was war, and I said: I'm going to shoot it again! [...] **it dawned on them that this girl, this broad [...] she won't give up, not [...] that she isn't a small woman**. (Maysaloun Hamoud)

Men's underestimation of women's efficacy can lead to a precious loss of time. Bat-Adam is an extremely accomplished and prolific filmmaker and the winner of Israel Prize for cinema who started making movies in 1979; Hamoud won the NETPAC Award for World or International Asian Film Premiere for her first feature film in 2016. Both Bat-Adam and Hamoud's narratives demonstrate the reluctance of their staff to receive and carry out their directions. In Bat-Adam's account, the time wasted squabbling over the size of the lens or the height of the camera is

---

2   A local council in the Northern District of Israel, where most inhabitants are Arab-Muslims.

only hinted at. In Hamoud's description, it is clear that the cameraman's countermanding her directions forced her to go on an additional day trip of shooting in the village with the crew, incurring an additional investment of time, labor, and money.

The effect of negative attitudes and stereotypes is also reflected in the words of the director, screenwriter, and cinematographer Esti Almo Wexler, whose filmography has depicted, inter alia, stories of the Ethiopian Jews and their lives in Israel.

> **It's like there's sack of images and stereotypes heaped on your back.** I was in a pitch meeting at the Haifa Film Festival [...] when a director comes to me and says: 'I want to tell you, I'm really proud of you, that you're going to direct films' [...] and he says, 'seriously, like, how did you come up with the idea?' Like, what do you mean how did you come up with the idea? [...] **it was as if he were speaking of himself, saying 'It's obvious why I'd be a director because I'm an Ashkenazi[3] man, I had tons of role models as directors, whereas you, where did you ever get the idea to be a director?'** (Esti Almo Wexler)

Similar to the way in which the glass ceiling becomes thicker and more impenetrable when additional social markers intersect, Almo Wexler depicts a celluloid ceiling which represents not only a gender-based form of discrimination but one that is simultaneously ethnically-based as well. While Almo Wexler does not talk directly about the element of wasted time, her description of a "sack of images and stereotypes" heaped on her back portrays a heavy burden that can slow down a woman on her way.

Men's disbelief in female efficacy, aptly encapsulated in the memorable quip, "never underestimate a man's ability to underestimate a woman"[4] (Paretsky 2009), has concrete material underpinnings:

---

3   Jews descendent from European and Western countries that are considered part of the Israeli elite.

4   The sentence, was also prominently featured in a Kathleen Turner 1991 film of the same title.

When I arrived at the Israeli film service, they asked: 'so [...] you're married?' I said I was. 'Got kids?' I do. 'What do you need all this for, anyway? Go to the kitchen, cook [...]' in these very words. I said: 'Yeah, great, thanks.' I went and came back and got things going. I had a hard time getting money. I'm like a merry-go-round, which is why most of my films really were low budget. **And I think women are seen as less capable of making a film. Give *her* millions? Millions?! There's nothing to do about it. A male industry. A men's club, you might say.** A lot of deals are closed in – pardon me – men's toilets. They stand there and [...] they close deals. It's true that now, here and there you see more women [...] like, they'll say we need a woman for the board of directors, so let's find someone. But generally, given the choice, I think they'd put 90% men there, or only men, anyway. Today it's as if it's become correct to always have a few women, but none of it's natural, it doesn't emerge from the inside, it's not what you'd call "intrinsic". It's because we're obliged to show we're actually inclusive and egalitarian. (Tzipi Tropé)

When I waited for a response from the film council if they'll support my film, there was someone else, another filmmaker who also had a project in the same year [...] and it was clear to me that it's either me or her. [...] if they select four projects, say, it was obvious that they'd place us on the same slot. **The woman's slot. And suddenly I told her, why the heck are we even on the same slot? Our projects are just so, so different, and yet, I knew clearly, that it'll be either me or her. And it was.** (Talya Lavie)

Throughout the years, the women's identities were marked identities. As a result, women won less grants and competed over a single grant predesignated to 'women'. According to the Israeli "Celluloid Ceiling" project (Elefant et al. 2021), the number of male directors who received support far outweighed female directors. For example, 121 male directors received support from the Rabinovich foundation, compared to 22 female directors. From the Israeli Film Foundation, 51 male directors received support, compared to 13 female ones (Elefant et al. 2021). This stark gender divergence is due, in part, to the low number of women directors who submit requests to the foundations. This is an example, then, of how inequality reproduces itself: Less women receive grants, so less women submit requests due to a belief that their chances are low. It is hard to make a film without a budget, especially a feature film, and it is even harder to promote it. This, in turn, leads many women directors to either expend energies on time-consuming bids to secure a budget with the odds stacked against them, or to resorting to make films without them.

Experiences of sexism and sexual harassment were rarely detailed or raised during the interviews conducted as part of the film. Yet, director Julie Shles spoke to the atmosphere in work meetings at some length:

> If you look at the beginning of Channel 2, at "Reshet"[5], it was like coming to some army base, you know, the way all those honchos strutted around there. It was an entirely different atmosphere. It was like [...] one long harassment. It'd start the moment we parked the car, there'd be this feeling that the two chicks have arrived, I had a production company with Amit Bruyar back then, and they'd talk to us that way. I mean, the way they talk to me in the street today: "redhead". Real vulgar, too, like, comments about your boobs and your ass. And that, too, was the atmosphere. And all sorts of "secretaries" would sit on their laps. It was something more resonant of the army, in the way that you either fight it out, or you allow a kind of fear, a fear that is all yours, not external, that makes you always try to carry favor, to let things slide, and he can talk to you in that way, and you just giggle [...] you come to a work meeting and its like [...] they just talk in the most [...] "suck my cock", like [...] (Julie Shles)

The sexist atmosphere Shles describes was familiar to other women filmmakers who had meetings in the same places she describes and encountered the same people. The aspect of fear Shles talks about as one possible reaction to these encounters is familiar to many women in the public

---

5   Israeli free-to-air television channel.

sphere and in the workplace. Feminist literature describes fear as a common result of patriarchal spaces in which a sexist atmosphere reinforces women's exclusion from public life. The fear is real, because women are forced to acclimatize themselves to spaces in which they may well become victims of sexual assault. The MeToo movement across the world and in Israel has done much to expose, in unprecedented detail, the endemic culture of sexual harassment and assaults that the film and television industry harbors. The accusations leveled by numerous women in the industry, including some against the erstwhile CEO of one of the Israeli television channels and against leading actors and figures in the industry, involved women directors who did not speak about these issues in the film. Yet their testimonies echo Shles' account and, like her, point to a broad phenomenon that everyone was aware of and kept silent about. Despite the possible impact of fear on workplace behaviors, the literature on this subject remains relatively scarce; however, one prominent well-discussed outcome of fear is that of silence (Kish-Gephart et al. 2009). In view of the importance of voice to the creative process, in terms of time, fear is one of the greatest impediments to action as it is commonly accompanied by stagnation and carries with it an implicit bias against creativity (Lee, Chang, and Choi 2017).

"Did you check up on the state of your ovaries"?

Motherhood has often been described as a social expectation of parenting directed uniquely at women, one that includes childbearing, care work, and housekeeping:

> Many **extremely talented women never reach the top of the pyramid, never direct – not because of a lack of talent, but because of cultural and social circumstances**. Because of the burden they place on us [...] I think that a woman's largest enemy in her creative life is herself. **It's this fear, it's this thing that she'd internalized from a very young age, this education to motherhood and the holy goal of starting a family – that keeps a lot of very talented women from a lot of jobs, including**

cinema [...]. There are a lot of woman editors because you can work it into family routines. A woman editor can still raise her children and work. It'd be really difficult for a camerawoman. She'd need to wake up at 4 AM, and what then? Who'll get up at 4 AM to prepare food for the kids? The man?? (Tova Ascher)

Film director and editor Asher's claims are corroborated by data that points to a very small percentage of camerawomen versus woman editors in the film industry (Elefant et al. 2021). Similarly, film director Keren Yedaya points to the biological clock as a unique challenge for women when they plan their careers:

A lot of women in the industry talk to me because **they're just at that 30–35-year-old range when they first get an opportunity to do a full-feature length film. And then they need to decide if they take the risk of letting the age of fertility pass and make a film, or do it before, or after.** And I find myself in all these appointments sort of offering [...] **how old are you exactly? Did you check up on the state of your ovaries?** First things first, then, get them checked and see if you have a year to spare, and if you do, go shoot first, because it's better to shoot first and then have a kid, [...]. It's not simple, not simple at all. You can't be pregnant, nor be with a little child. I mean, it's technically impossible to shoot when you're pregnant. (Keren Yedaya)

Having children also becomes a continuous looming threat to one's career, especially when calculating whether to take a risk is necessary, such as taking up work abroad:

The film ("Newland") premiered in the Jewish Film Festival in Los Angeles, and I think it was the most talked-about premier back then [...] and after the screening [...] the crowd cheered and actually gave a standing ovation, and agents from a talent agency approached me and offered to sign me, which back then represented Mick Jagger and Barbara Streisand [...]. The next day I met them in an office, they gave me a contract and I signed it without even reading it, and I was so excited, so dazed, and they soon sent me a Hollywood script and an offer to direct [...] and then the moment of truth came, I had to inform them when I was coming, and I didn't go. It's also because **I was scared [...] And I've got the children with me, in a foreign environment, and they were so little. What'll I do? What'll I do with them? How will I get by?** I guess if I were a man, I'd go to Hollywood, and I'd direct the film, who wouldn't want such an opportunity? If there are sliding doors, that was a sliding door moment. I mean, I stayed in Israel [...]. I didn't become a Hollywood director. (Orna Ben-Dor)

The fear aspect that film and television director Orna Ben-Dor describes here is materialized in her self-doubt of her ability to get by with small children in an unfamiliar environment, and one she identifies as unique to women. Ben-Dor speaks of a formative life and career choice, a path she chose not to take despite having the opportunity to do so, by referring to the film *Sliding Doors* (dir. Peter Howitt 1998). Ben-Dor's evocation can be seen as testimony to the significance she accords to the event. Possibly, it also suggests that, to some degree, she weighs her life against an image of what could have been, and who she could have become, had she accepted the offer.

Discussion

In conceptualizing the challenges that women face in the industry as measurable by time, the findings depicted numerous forms of gender-based discriminations that women directors faced that prevented them from advancing their careers as they saw fit. Focusing our analysis on the issue of lost time leads us to suggest that, by itself, the metaphor of the "Celluloid Ceiling" (Lauzen 2011) comes short of fully conceptualizing the extent of the obstacles women face in the film industry. We do not offer to replace this important concept, rather to build on it by suggesting an additional metaphor of "Celluloid Hurdles" – a series of diverse barriers and obstacles that women uniquely face, and which often prevents or delays them in the ongoing race to make a movie.

In this manner, it is possible to speak not only of the additional 44 Israeli women film director who have created a feature film by 2020 and were not interviewed in Zamir's film, but also of all the women who have attended a film school but never had the opportunity to direct – precisely because of the numerous obstacles that are depicted in the interviews. Calling attention to the fact that all the women within the data set had successfully overcome some of the hurdles and made at least one feature film. Hence, they represent the group of successful, well-selected Israeli women film directors, who have made it against all odds. Nonetheless, by way of expanding on the notion of Celluloid Hurdles, we invoke four additional metaphors which capture specific axes that intersect time, cinema, and gender: "uncertain time", "time loop", "sliding doors" and "time standing still". Finally, we also chose to address "gendered histori-cal time", which, in this case, accounts for the positive cumulative aspect of time as gender equality in women's representation in the film industry edges closer.

- **Uncertain Time**: the loss of valuable time as the outcome of low self-efficacy among women and the low efficacy ascribed by a male-dom-inated environment. As a result, decades might pass by until woman filmmakers make their first film. "Uncertain time" also captures the silenced voices we have not examined here and includes the many women who dropped out from film schools, as well as those who have but never succeeded in creating a feature-length film.
- **The Time Loop**: lost time due to the need to reshoot or re-create footage as a result of a gender-sensitive intransigence on behalf of the male crew to adhere to the directives of the woman director, either due to a sense they have of knowing better than she does, or a reluctance to carry out instructions given by a woman. This appeared in some of the interviews but was not pervasive. Still, this phenomenon is widely recorded in the literature as well, pointing to men's unwillingness to receive orders from women or accept their leadership as legitimate (Watson 1988).
- **The Sliding Doors**: women who had opportunities they could not make the most of, or women who faced a choice at a particular point in their lives whether to focus on raising a child or making a movie. Unlike the film of the same title (*Sliding Doors* by dir. Peter

Howitt 1998) that presents the two alternatives simultaneously, this situation points to an imaginary alternative life that looms over one's actual life and casts it as incomplete.

- **Time Standing Still:** experiences of gender-based discrimination and of harassment and sexual assault, whether they occur in specific moments or are ingrained in a misogynistic work-culture, sear themselves onto memory causing a sense of threat and fear. The interviewees tended to speak more about experiences of gender-based discrimination than about sexual harassment. Yet, many of them mentioned fear as related to gender inequality. It is important to note that fear leads to stagnation and impedes the creative drive (Lee et al. 2017). Moreover, sexual abuse has been extensively raised in the professional literature and in other interviews given by women directors – including some of the same interviewees who appear in Zamir's film – who did speak about harassment they had endured working in the film industry. The mere absence of this topic from the current film could possibly represent the decision of the film director herself, who chose not to focus on this topic. Even though life continues, exposure to such violence leads to mental scarring and can cause mental disorders such as panic and compulsive self-deprecation, which only further aggravate the isolation of the female creator subjected to the harassment. Research on the negative post-factum effects of sexual harassment and violence recorded numerous symptoms, such as depression, anxiety, post-traumatic stress disorder, self-blame, self-doubt, low self-esteem, self-confidence, and suicidal thoughts. This time-standing-still aspect, in which victims endure psychic scarring, manifests itself in victim's professional lives as well, with studies recording heightened levels of disengagement from work, increased feelings of burn-out, and a diminishing sense of fulfillment in, and commitment to, working life (Zhang et al. 2020).
- **Gendered Historical Time**: alongside time wasted overcoming the numerous celluloid fences that women face, the linear axis of historical time represents a hopeful vision for the future and casts time as an enabler and agent of change. This linear model of time points

to a generational shift taking place that is creating significant transitions for women. The past first appears as a time when oppression of women meant they did not dare to want things or to clearly formulate their professional aspirations, which implies an implicit understanding of reality as unchangeable, and a sense of disappointment about miscarried careers. It later depicts the generation of pioneering women filmmakers who spoke of their isolation as women in the industry. The present, however, is a time when many women are joining the industry, their examples de-exceptionalize women directors and cast a positive effect on aspiring women filmmakers' self-efficacy and self-belief. Historical time is also expressed on a private level, in the personal development and maturation that women described as enabling and enriching to the creative process.

In sum, the universal time measured in watches and clocks across the globe ticks differently for women in the film industry. Overt and covert obstacles that not everybody overcomes make the way impossible for some and longer for others. Taking into account various outcomes of ageism towards older directors in the Israeli film industry (Aharoni Lir and Ayalon 2022) these obstacles that delay women's career as directors potentially hold severe future prices, such as greater difficulties in fund raising. And yet, on the historical scale of things, both collectively and personally, a change is slowly taking place. We did not engage in this study with the cinematic stories that women directors bring to the screen. These stories are important as they depict round female characters and represent the perspectives of women of different positionalities on life. It seems that we, too, are stuck in a loop, one that forces us to speak about the challenges involved in telling a story instead of the story itself.

References

Aharoni Lir, Shlomit, and Liat Ayalon."The wounded lion – ageism and masculinity in the Israeli film industry". *Frontiers in Psychology* 13 (2022). https://doi.org/10.3389/fpsyg.2022.756472.

Benjamin, Orly. "Gender in Israel: new studies on gender in the Yishuv and the State." (2012): 176–183 (Hebrew).

Boyatzis, Richard. E. *Transforming qualitative information: Thematic analysis and code development.* Thousand Oaks, CA: Sage, 1998.

Braun, Virginia, and Victoria Clarke. "Using thematic analysis in psychology." *Qualitative research in psychology* 3.2 (2006): 77–101.

Cerrato, Javier, and Eva Cifre. "Gender inequality in household chores and work-family conflict." *Frontiers in psychology* 9 (2018): 1330.

Cotter, David, Joan Hermsen, Seth Ovadia, and Reeve Vanneman. "The glass ceiling effect." *Social forces* 80.2 (2001): 655–681.

Denzin, Norman, and Yvonna Lincoln. *Handbook of qualitative research.* London: Sage Publications, 1994.

Elefant, Lior, Etty Konor-Attias, Yael Hasson, and Noga Dagan-Buzaglo. *The Celluloid Ceiling: A Gendered Perspective on the Division of Labor, Awards and Grants in Israeli Cinema.* Tel Aviv: Adva Center, 2021.

Fogel-Bizawi, Sylvie. "Families in Israel: Between familarity and Postmodernism." *Sex, Gender, Politics.* Eds. Israeli Dafna., Friedman Ariella., Dahan Kaleb, Henriette. Herzog, Hanna. Hassan, Manar. Nave, Hannah. & Fogel-Bizawi, Sylvie. Tel-Aviv: Red Line, 1999. 106–166.

Gilligan, Carol. *In a Different Voice: Psychological Theory and Women's Development.* Cambridge, MA: Harvard University Press, 2016 [1982].

Howitt, Peter. *Sliding Doors.* 1998.

Kish-Gephart, Jennifer J., James R. Detert, Linda Klebe Treviño and Amy C. Edmondson, "Silenced by fear: The nature, sources, and consequences of fear at work." *Research in Organizational Behavior* 29 (2009): 163–193. https://doi.org/10.1016/j.riob.2009.07.002.

Lauzen, Martha. "Research Center for the Study of Women in Television & Film". https://womenintvfilm.sdsu.edu/

Lauzen, Martha. *The Celluloid Ceiling: Behind-the-Scenes Employment of Women on the Top 250 Films of 2010*. Center for the Study of Women in Television and Film, 2011.

Lee, Young Soo, Jae Yoon Chang, and Jin Nam Choi. "Why reject creative ideas? Fear as a driver of implicit bias against creativity." *Creativity Research Journal* 29(3) (2017): 225–235.

Lyden, John. "Half the picture." *Journal of Religion & Film*, 22.1 (2018): Article 13.

Meece, Judith, Beverly Bower Glienke, and Samantha Burg. "Gender and motivation." *Journal of school psychology* 44.5 (2006): 351–373.

Paretsky, Sara. *Blood Shot: A VI Warshawski Novel*. New York: Delacorte Press, 2009.

Pfefferman, Talia. Speaking "Silence of a woman speaking: women's silence, speech and action according to 'My Life in the Country' (1935), by Hania Pekelman". *Gender in Israel: New Studies on Gender in the Yishuv and the State*. Eds, Shilo Margalit and Katz Gideon. The Ben-Gurion Institute for the Study of Israel and Zionism at Ben-Gurion University of the Negev (2011): A, 23–49 (Hebrew).

Ragin, Charles, and Lisa Amoroso. *Constructing social research* (2 ed.). Thousand Oaks: Sage, 2011.

Shaer-Meoded, Israela. "The Unknown Cinema: On Early Women's Cinema in Israel (1969–1983)." Tel Aviv University: MA dissertation, 2016 (Hebrew).

Tzameret, Hagar, Naomi Chazan, Hanna Herzog, Yulia Basin, Ronna Brayer-Garb, Hadass Ben Eliyahu. *The Gender Index 2021 – Gender Inequality in Israel*. Jerusalem: Van Leer Institute Press. 2021.

Watson, Carol. "When a Woman is the Boss: Dilemmas in Taking Charge." *Group & Organization Studies* 13.2 (1988): 163–181.

Zamir, Smadar. *In the Director's Chair Sits a Woman*. 2020.

Zhang, Dafang., Pistorio, A. L., Payne, D., & Lifchez, S. D. Promoting gender equity in the# MeToo Era. *The Journal of Hand Surgery* 45.12 (2020): 1167–1172.

"Be the Captain they remember"
Fandom Responses to Ageing *Star Trek* Protagonists

Isabella Hesse

Abstract: *This virtual ethnography focuses on fan responses to the SF drama series Star Trek: Picard and its ageing cast. The revival of a popular SF franchise after a pause of almost two decades, the reprise of iconic roles by visibly transformed cast members and the ensuing discussions in online spaces yield an insight into viewers' attitudes towards representations of age and ageing in popular culture. Drawing on a qualitative analysis of posts in a Facebook group dedicated to the series, this article maps out dominant cultural narratives on ageing and the meaning that fans ascribe to Star Trek: Picard within this landscape. Commentary on the ageing bodies of actors and actresses reveals what some fans consider "graceful" or "successful" ageing. Praise of those who are perceived to have aged "like a fine wine" demonstrates appreciation of older bodies, while reinforcing pressure to maintain attractiveness. Furthermore, online fan discourses show a marked discrepancy in the way male and female attractiveness are discussed, with female stars being continually objectified and sexualized. Conversations on characters' transformations over time often revolve around expectations of continuity and age-appropriateness. Significant changes to a franchise can challenge fans' sense of affective ownership. While ageing bears negative connotations of decline and decreased autonomy, some fans were inspired by Star Trek: Picard's depiction of ageing. The meaning of "ageing well" emerged as successfully managing change, staying true to oneself while still integrating the inevitable changes wrought by time rather than denying them.*

Keywords: *ageing; fandom; Star Trek; gender; cultural gerontology; fan studies; aca/fan; virtual ethnography; intersectionality; SF*

Introduction – Age, the Final Frontier?

In 2020, the iconic character Jean-Luc Picard, played by then 80-year-old Sir Patrick Stewart, returned to television screens for the first time in almost 20 years. In the SF drama *Star Trek: Picard*, interplanetary travel is commonplace, holograms can function as crew of a star ship and hot Earl Grey tea materializes out of nothing with a simple voice command. But one aspect, that *Picard*'s world at the eve of the twenty-fifth century shares with our present, is that people still grow old. With season two having aired in 2022, *Picard* forms part of a revival of the *Star Trek* franchise which began with *Star Trek: Discovery* in 2017. In the pilot episode of *Picard*, we meet the titular character, not onboard a star ship but tending to a vineyard in his retirement. When his assistant urges him to "Be the Captain they remember" ("Remembrance", 1.1), she echoes the expectations of many viewers. By analysing posts in online fan spaces about the transformation of well-known *Trek* characters and actors, I gained a better understanding of how these viewers interpret pop-cultural representations of ageing. Old age in popular culture is typically depicted through stereotyping – frail bodies and senile minds. However, due to a growing demographic of consumers past middle age, there is a trend towards catering to older audiences with more multifaceted depictions (Jones and Batchelor 2015, xii). Cultural gerontologists have identified age-as-decline as a dominant cultural narrative and developed a variety of counternarratives (Gullette 2004, 11). Some narratives centre defying age by maintaining a fit, youthful, attractive body, but this focus on individual strategies obscures underlying power relations and fundamentally reinforces the equation of age-as-decline (Laceulle 2018, 81, Katz and Calasanti 2015, 30). My research showcases another facet of ageing narratives, by asking people to consider ageing well in relation to fictional characters and celebrities they cherish or look up to. Commenters weighed the relatability of vulnerable ageing protagonists against aspirational age-defying heroes. While there was no unified consensus on what ageing well entails, fans agreed that transformations must uphold the continuity of the story universe.

This article pays special attention to intersections of ageism and sexism. As outlined by essayist Susan Sontag (1972), patriarchal societies are more lenient towards male ageing, while women are held to a higher standard of beauty and subsequently suffer for failing to meet that standard in later life (30). Women have been chided as tools of the patriarchy for striving to adhere to sexist and ageist beauty standards but have also been framed as empowered for succeeding within this framework (Hurd Clarke and Bennett 2015, 134). The burden of choosing how to present themselves lies with women, who can only hope to minimize criticism and objectification, but not escape it, as their worth in a patriarchal society is so closely bound to their looks. The experiences of actresses from previous *Star Trek* shows reprising their roles alongside Stewart, including Jeri Ryan as Seven of Nine and Marina Sirtis as Deanna Troi, reflect this double standard.

Researching as an Aca/Fan

My approach is modelled after sociologist Christine Hine's definition of virtual ethnography as an immersive, multi-modal, and multi-sited ethnographic method (2016, 22–25). 'The' internet is not a single research field, but rather consists of various sites and contexts, which are interconnected with life offline and with each other. These enable varying practices and forms of discourse. According to Hine, the virtual ethnographer constructs their own field through "choices about which connections to follow rather than through tracing out a pre-existing location" (2016, 26). For me, this meant centring my research on a private Facebook group with roughly 20,000 members, then following links and references within the group to other sites, such as the subreddit r/startrekpicard. The group functioned as a semi-private, semi-public forum, since only group members could see posts, but most members were not anonymous and shared their 'offline' names, faces and personal information on their profile pages. This group, where posts and comments were subject to clearly articulated rules, yielded more polite and restrained interactions than on more anonymous sites.[1] For instance, the moderator who gave me permission to pose research questions to the Facebook group requested that I monitor responses for 'hate'-comments, signalling that an effort was being made to cultivate a harmonious atmosphere. Fortunately, my questions prompted 16 responses expressing enthusiasm, frustration and frequently ambivalence, but no hate speech.[2] To protect the privacy of group members, comments will be quoted using pseudonyms and without direct links to the posts in question.

Taking a step back, why study *Star Trek* in the first place? A good deal of scholarship has been devoted to mapping the extensive *Star Trek* franchise, which now spans almost 60 years. This intergenerational reach is part of my motivation for conducting this research. My mother and I both grew up watching *Star Trek: The Original Series* with our families. While we both identify as fans, we practice fandom in different ways, we have different interpretations of characters, and we laugh at different memes. As literary scholar Janice Radway describes in her 1984 study of romance readers, consumers of the same media text can form various interpretive communities with variable literacies. Furthermore, she argues that "[i]nterpretive communities may not simply differ over what to do with metaphors and tropes; they may disagree even more fundamentally over the nature and purpose of reading itself" (Radway 1984, 54). This article does not aim to explain what the 'average' *Star Trek* fan thinks, since *Star Trek* audiences are a heterogeneous group. Some attend

---

1   From the group's 'about' page: "This is a positive themed group, we don't ignore the bad or the awful, but we just don't focus on it, we want the show to be successful, and get as many seasons as fate will allow us and as many spin-off shows and or movies as we can get out of this fantastic franchise."

2   I posted an explanation of my research interest as a student of cultural anthropology and fellow fan, along with these questions: "How do you feel about actors returning to their characters years later? What do you think about how the topic of age is treated in the story of *Picard's* first season? What does it mean to age 'well' or 'gracefully' in your opinion?"

conventions, some watch and re-watch favourite episodes while others write an academic paper about *Star Trek*.

Similar to fan scholar Henry Jenkins, I confess to being an aca/fan, a "hybrid identity" combining a fan's perspective and an academic one (2006, 4). Positioning myself as an aca/fan and attempting what Jenkins describes as an "insider approach to media ethnography", requires transparency and reflection of what this dual perspective brought to the table, whether it was advantageous or not (2006, 4). As a fan, I can follow online conversations without additional research into worldbuilding or terminology. However, my perspective is also informed by nostalgia, since characters like Spock, Uhura, and Picard were heroes of my childhood. My relationship to *Star Trek* has always been entwined with my evolving knowledge of and identification with feminism. I hold expectations that *Star Trek* stories should promote accepting, indeed celebrating difference. So, I entered my virtual field site keenly attuned to sexism among fans, and perhaps somewhat defensive of my own interpretation of the franchise's core values, which can be summed up by the in-universe axiom: "Infinite Diversity in Infinite Combinations" (Memory Alpha). Writing this article required a conscious effort to make room for critical analysis to exist beside nostalgia.

My material consists mostly of single comments, as well as one longer exchange with a group member, a self-described "walking Sir Patrick lexicon" who goes by "Mr. Picard".[3] Even as an aca/fan, much of Mr Picard's specialized knowledge about the actors and behind the scenes processes of *Star Trek: Picard* was new to me. Despite focusing on just a small portion of the vast online *Star Trek* fandom, my research turned up intense disagreement within this group. Mr. Picard shared that he has left other Facebook groups in which "too much hate and misinformation" were being spread and has blocked users for discriminatory and homophobic content. The negativity towards new entries into the franchise, above all the harsh criticism of attempts to make *Star Trek* more diverse by including queer characters and characters of

---

3   Our conversation in German has been translated for this publication.

colour, has strongly impacted his enjoyment of fandom spaces. Encountering bigoted or hateful posts in fandom spaces is disheartening, but in the interest of not sweeping unpleasant aspects of fandom under the carpet, let me make two important distinctions. Firstly, anger towards 'nuTrek' needs to be contextualized within broader current discourses on the role of representation and political correctness within pop-culture – this is not a problem unique to *Star Trek*. Secondly, as Mr. Picard explained based on his experience in various online spaces, hyperbolic hate can be a tool to drive engagement with content, get more clicks and, therefore, more advertising revenue (Mr. Picard, 19 August 2021). Further research could investigate the ways in which online platforms provide incentives for media criticism to escalate. Although it would be fascinating to explore many kinds of *Star Trek* fandom, this case study in virtual ethnography remains in orbit around one specific online community of fans. Perhaps future studies can seek out new groups and boldly go where no ethnographer has gone before.

Ageing "Like a Fine Wine"

Members of the Facebook group frequently posted pictures of *Star Trek* cast-members in or out of character, which were then showered with appreciative comments and heart emojis. These posts indicated the tone of interaction cultivated in this specific group. Rather than concluding that there is no derision or dislike towards the ageing physicality of *Star Trek* actors, I observed that to this group of fans it was important to express a positive attitude towards actors and characters. But this appreciation did not take place in a vacuum and can be seen as a reaction to widespread ageist discourses that ascribe decline, frailty, and a loss of attractiveness to growing old (Gullette 2004, 8). After all, there would be no need to explicitly comment that Sir Patrick Stewart is handsome "with hair or bald" or that he has "aged like a fine wine" if there were no latent expectation of decline. Additionally, appreciative comments were often paired with humorous self-deprecation ("my knees would never allow for that pose"). Photos of Stewart with his wife Sunny Ozell (who is 43) provoked both compliments and light mockery. While some envied the "gorgeous couple" and Stewart, who "still rocks it", a joke about Stewart having "married his nurse?" implied an inappropriate age-imbalance. This comment presupposes not only that age entails frailty, but also employs the stereotype that care work is women's work. Still, relationships of older men with younger women are far more normalized than the reverse (Sontag 1972, 36–37). As critical gerontologists Toni Calasanti and Neal King (2015) write: "[T]he ways in which people mark or perceive bodies as 'old' vary with gender, race, class, and sexuality. For instance, women, accorded status in part for their sexual attractiveness to men, appear to be old at younger ages than do men" (196). I encountered comments about Marina Sirtis and Jeri Ryan that expressed a sexual fantasy, as well as innuendo-laden jokes ("I'd *still* bang it lad lol" [emphasis mine], "jerry ryan in a cat suit ooooh yeeeah" [sic]). There was no similarly proprietary or overtly sexual tone in comments on male actors. Jeri Ryan's costume changes, from a skin-tight catsuit in the late 90s and early 2000s to a less sexualized, more rugged outfit in *Picard*, was bemoaned by some, but deemed more appropriate by others. Ryan's clothes, body, appearance, and by extension her age, are treated as a core aspect of her character, while Captain Picard's clothes and appearance are treated as more incidental. Stewart may be called "handsome" or "sexy" by his admirers, but his character is not discussed time and time again with regards to sex appeal. Using Sylvia Spruck Wrigley's detailed examination of age in *Star Trek*, the discrepancy can be traced back to the *The Original Series* (2022, 423–424). In the 1967 episode "The Deadly Years" (2.11), members of the Enterprise crew find themselves rapidly ageing. While Captain Kirk and his senior officers primarily struggle with deteriorating physical and mental capability, the one female crewmember afflicted is the one most upset by how she looks. But filmmaking has come a long way since 1967. An interview with Marina Sirtis and Brent Spiner highlights how the former perceives the oft-cited double standard of ageing (Sontag 1972):

SIRTIS: [T]he man who invented that high-definition camera – and it was a man, because a woman would have never fucking invented

> it, excuse my French. May he rot in hell for all eternity!
> SPINER: Right. But see, in my case: CGI… so I look fine!
> SIRTIS: Yeah, it's all right for you, Mr. Android, the rest of us look like something the cat dragged in… (Sirtis and Spiner 2020)

Sirtis' exclamation implies that women are more conscious of a need to hide flaws in their appearances and are subjected to greater pressure to do so. The tone of this interview is light-hearted, but losing work-opportunities due to ageing is a serious concern. The sf drama *Advantageous* (2015) offers a dystopian deconstruction of where a cultural obsession with youth and beauty may lead. Struggling to provide for herself and her daughter, *Advantageous'* protagonist must subject herself to a risky new medical procedure to attain a younger body. In addition to physical agony, she suffers the erasure of her identity, the humiliation and rejection of having her 'less-marketable' traits, including her race, overwritten with a conventionally beautiful young, white face. *Advantageous'* intersectional critique of how ageism pits women against one another and exploits the desperation of those whose "erotic or cultural currency" is beginning to wane, grows more relevant as digital de-ageing continues to develop (Hurd Clarke and Bennett 2015, 134).

The pressure of ageing appropriately was felt by female members of the fan group as well:

> As I age, going from single woman, to married, to mom, and now grandmother I have asked myself what image I am trying to maintain, what makes for "graceful ageing"? I have tried to stay healthy and young looking. My husband appreciates that, but I need to do that for my own mental health. I feel better when I look better. I have to balance that with what is age appropriate. No tattoos, nose rings or revealing clothing can really disguise that I am 58. I feel the same about my favourite characters on Trek. I am thrilled to see them age, but I don't want to see them become worthless couch potatoes, or cringe-worthy for trying too hard to be young and cool. (Margaret, 18 August 2021)

The phrasing here connotes a sense of obligation. Calasanti and King (2015) explain that ageing individuals are often held responsible for fighting off the effects of time, as though ageing were a moral deficiency: "If people control their health, and others can infer that health from how their bodies look, then those who appear unhealthy and old can be seen to deserve their exclusion" (196). To further complicate the situation, denying one's own age was also described as inappropriate: "Ageing gracefully as an actor is like De Niro, or Pacino. They take on roles that fit their stage in life. Ageing badly is Tom Cruise. How many 60-year-Olds still jump motorcycles?" (Anthony, 18 August 2021) These comments evoke a sense of a delicate balance. How is one meant to satisfy demands to be active, to take responsibility for maintaining one's health, so as not to be "worthless", but simultaneously accept one's limitations with "grace, humility and dignity"? How to know when you are "trying too hard" or need to try harder? Commenting on a photo of Jeri Ryan with "53 and still beautiful" might be intended as a compliment, but it also reinforces the ageist equation of age as decline, decay, and deficiency. Such comments present celebrities as aspirational while exerting subtle pressure by suggesting that they are still beloved *because* they have succeeded in not ageing too visibly. As Sontag (1972) has observed, these exceptions "do not challenge the rule" (36). Failures are sanctioned with ridicule or speculation about plastic surgery. Ultimately, while this group of fans directed positivity towards the ageing bodies of *Trek*-actors, ageing "like a fine wine" emerged as a result of managing one's age with care, effort, and dignity. In other words, ageing well is not attainable for everyone. Cultural gerontologist Margaret Cruikshank (2013) has pointed out that modern societies value self-determination without accounting for the social inequalities which it is contingent upon, treating older people as though they were a homogeneous group with equal resources to manage ageing (10). As an alternative, Cruikshank suggests "comfortable" ageing. By becoming aware of the "social forces" at play in ageing, older people can be liberated from the individual responsibility to defy age. Perhaps this process, which Cruikshank (2013) calls "learning to be old", could make the tightrope of age-appropriateness a bit easier to balance on (210).

Mind the Brand Gap

Star Trek: Picard does not shy away from showing the iconic Captain as a changed man. In the very first episode, we learn that Picard has resigned in protest from Starfleet ("Remembrance", 1.1). His age and faded relevance are repeatedly emphasized – the receptionist at Starfleet headquarters does not recognize him, he takes his favourite tea decaf, he is called "a relic" and "mothballed" ("Maps and Legends", 1.2). The first season forces its protagonist to face his mortality head on, while the second deals with Picard coming to terms with emotional wounds from his childhood. *Picard*'s depiction of the challenges of ageing, whether played for laughs or drama, resonated strongly with some fans' personal experiences. Joe explained becoming aware of his own nostalgia and idealization of Picard, a bittersweet coming to terms with change:

> I've said it before here in this group: getting to see these people again felt like home. It was a family reunion. Picard had aged and he still had that passion and intrigue we knew and loved but it was like getting to see your own Father, who for you as a kid growing up was the strongest, bravest, wisest, and then seeing him aged and now you are the adult… Does that make sense? Picard was the same man. But you got to see his fragility too. (Joe, 18 August 2021)

Commenters on the subreddit r/startrekpicard – which, unlike the Facebook group, did not nudge members towards positive posting – took a bleaker view of the characters' transformation. One described the aged Picard as an uncomfortable reminder of the fate that awaits everyone. Another, who mentioned watching the show with their father, found Picard's dismissal at Starfleet headquarters in the show emblematic of the disrespect with which older people are treated in the present.

Looking at more melancholic responses begs the question of how much change is too much change? Reviving a franchise or story bears the risk of causing controversy. Media scholar Matt Hills uses the term "brand gap" to describe the discrepancy felt by fans of the series *Twin Peaks*, whose expectations were drastically challenged by the show's revival (2018, 317). Briefly stepping into the neutral zone of aca/fandom, I experienced a sense of "brand gap" myself when I watched the first episode of *Star Trek: Discovery* in 2017. The tone of the show was far darker and more cynical than I had expected. Though I overcame my disappointment and ended up enjoying *Discovery* more and more each season, I recall how jarring it was to turn on *Star Trek* expecting a hopeful vision of an sf utopia and see the protagonists bloodily stumble into war instead. I have found that many criticisms of *Picard* run along a similar line – the new series was breaking continuity to a degree that the universe and characters were unrecognizable: "Picard was a broken down wuss. This is not the man who kicked Son'a ass, not the man who gave the famous drumhead speech, or the speech about Data's rights, etc. And as for Seven? Clearly, she forgot everything she learned under Janeway because now she's a murdering vigilante." (r/startrekpicard) By referencing specific events from *Star Trek: The Next Generation* and *Star Trek: Voyager*, this commenter demonstrates a depth of knowledge and a strong emotional identification with the shows and characters. As Bethan Jones illustrates using the example of *X-Files* fans, this level of "affective ownership" may develop through intense investment of time, attention, and emotional energy in a media text (2017, 343). People who have spent years watching, reflecting on, and discussing *Star Trek*, who have perhaps spent money on merchandise, or created their own fan works, understandably develop a firm idea of what makes the beloved franchise good, and what a revival should look like (Jones 2017, 350). *Star Trek* has been a part of pop-culture since 1966, has been worked on and developed by scores of people, many of whom bridged the increasingly blurred fan-creator divide and helped to establish practices like fanfiction and conventions, which have since become cornerstones of fandom – is it any wonder that there is contention about what the *Star Trek* brand ought to be?

Mr. Picard mixes wit and frustration in his description of fan reactions to the 'new' Picard: "He's only wanted as a glowing never-ageing hero. Which he never was in TNG [*Star Trek: The Next Generation*] either, [...] but people just don't pay close attention. Sometimes I think they're watching a completely different series than I am" (Mr. Picard, 18 August 2021). This comment suggests that divergent interpretations are not exclusive to so-called 'nuTrek', but rather that arguments over the new series reveal previous divisions between interpretive communities. During our conversation, I was struck by Mr. Picard's careful distinction between himself as a fan of Sir Patrick and long-time lover of Jean-Luc Picard, and "the Trekkies": "I aged with Jean-Luc. I never saw him – unlike the Trekkies – as a static character whose story ended with *Nemesis* [the 2002 film]. For the Trekkies he remained that Jean-Luc and now they're shaken because he's suddenly so different for them." (Mr. Picard, 18 August 2021) To Mr. Picard it is clear that "Trekkies" are disappointed with the new series because they idolized Picard as a role model, while he has always seen Jean-Luc as fallible and changeable.

The consistent use of the character's first name corresponds with Mr. Picard's insistence that the role of "Captain" is just one aspect of the man, even a "mask" worn by Picard. This view of the character is not incompatible with the aged, frail, embittered Picard that other fans take issue with or are saddened by. So perhaps instead of asking how much change is too much, we ought to ask what makes some changes palatable? As a science-fiction series, *Star Trek: Picard* boasts a cast of characters who do not all age as ordinary humans do. In the case of the android Data, played by Brent Spiner, computer animation was used to make Spiner's appearance more like it was 18 years ago. In fact, Spiner is quoted as saying that CGI-technology was part of what convinced him to return to the role (Lovett 2020). Even so, some viewers were dissatisfied with Data's appearance:

> Getting to see Riker and Deanna again was a delight. Again, akin to a family reunion. I needed to see them. I needed to see my family. [...] Age was handled well in my opinion. It felt natural. These seemed like natural progressions. For Data's character – visually it was rather off-putting. But I understood the reason. I just wish more attention to detail could have been done. It was Data. But it wasn't Data all in the same breath. But I liked getting to revisit with him. (Joe, 18 August 2021)

While the ageing of humanoid characters felt like a "natural progression" to Joe, seeing a character who is supposed to be a machine age was "off-putting". Data and Brent Spiner were not given the same leeway to visibly age as other actors, because an aged Data troubles the continuity of the story universe. Given the heterogeneity of viewership, opinions are bound to diverge on how characters would 'naturally' develop over time. As the conversation with Mr. Picard demonstrates, some viewers are far more comfortable with embracing changes than others. Season two presented a similar conundrum with the return of Guinan and Q, played by Whoopi Goldberg and John de Lancie, two characters who were originally presented as ageless in *The Next Generation*. Though my research unfortunately concluded before season two aired, the fan group reacted to the announcement of Q's return with ambivalence similar to Joe's comment on Data. Many (myself included) were excited to see Q again, but wary of how his character might develop. When I asked group members how they would feel about Q being digitally de-aged, most replies favoured the character appearing older, but with a plausible in-universe explanation. Season two did just that, as both Guinan and Q's altered appearance was not ignored, but relevant to their respective subplots about personal growth.

Warts and All

Ageing well, ageing successfully, ageing gracefully – what do these ambiguous terms imply? Medical researcher John W. Rowe and psychologist and social scientist Robert L. Kahn outlined a medical framework of "successful ageing" which comprises maintaining physical and mental health as well as interpersonal relationships through making the 'correct' lifestyle choices (Rowe and Kahn 1997, 433). This model has become quite widely used but has been called into question by critical gerontologists more attuned to intersecting social inequalities (Katz and Calasanti 2015). Rowe and Kahn's emphasis on individuals' actions to fend off decline fails to address the injustice of marginalizing people whose physical, mental, or social wellbeing has decreased with age. Instead of questioning power relations which make certain demographics more vulnerable to illness or isolation than others, the model places responsibility on individual people to avoid negative consequences of age for as long as possible (Calasanti 2016, 1095). While members of the Facebook group did not cite "successful ageing" verbatim, I recognize elements of Rowe and Kahn's framework in their replies to my questions, mainly a desire to remain healthy and active instead of, to quote Margaret, "couch potatoes" (18 August 2021). Ageing gracefully was often associated with physical appearance, but some responders named non-physical attributes: "I think many long-time fans of *Star Trek* are getting older ourselves, so we enjoy seeing older characters portrayed as heroic, wise and active. Also, seeing people like Betty White, Mel Brooks and Dick Van Dyke who are still sharp and funny while pushing 100 gives one hope for your own future brain!" (Jonathan, 18 August 2021) Jonathan emphasised the feeling of ageing in tandem with an object of fandom, which illustrates how significant narratives can be as a source of inspiration for people entering old age.

Many commenters showed apprehension of ageing, explicitly or implicitly through phrases like "warts and all", but were nonetheless able to imagine ageing positively:

Ageing gracefully. That comment has never sat well with me. In my experience, those using this comment were judging older people's looks rather than looking at the person they have become. I like the term ageing well and to me that means being comfortable in your own skin, warts and all. It means accepting who you've become and continue to strive to be a person that people want to be around. (Susanna, 18 August 2021)

I think Picard's essence remained despite his frail voice. I admit that seeing him more frail and less tough looking as in TNG hit my heart. It reminded me of my own fears around vulnerability of the body and being old, not just older. But what compellingly stood out is the way Picard handled it with incredible grace, humility and dignity. He stood for an ideal, not his ego as THE great Picard with that tough body and mind. He played a softer, more emotional Picard. His greatness was in his character's humility and determination to do the honourable thing, that cool head despite the aching heart. Patrick Stewart is incredible. Stunning in fact. In an age where hon-

our is old fashioned, the way he played Picard made honour sexy
and relevant. (Sara, 6 December 2021)

Whether you focus more on the body or on personality, it would seem
based on these comments that self-acceptance and self-determination
are at the core of 'ageing well'. Health is not dependant on lifestyle
choices alone, as an individual can't control genetics or health care
infrastructure – but anyone can make the decision to strive for humour,
humility, or honour. Another fascinating aspect is how fan's criteria of
ageing well resemble the qualities which Sontag ascribes to conventional
masculinity: "[C]ompetence, autonomy, self-control – qualities which
the disappearance of youth does not threaten." (1972, 35) According to
Sontag, men can more easily accept the physical consequences of ageing
as part of human existence, while women as a "more *narrowly* defined
kind of human being" struggle to be seen (and see themselves) as worthy
separate from their fleeting beauty and sexual desirability (1972, 33). The
ideal of ageing well which commenters described to me included the
freedom to be judged by more than your looks.

    In an attempt to overcome the binary of age-as-decline and age-
defying narratives, philosopher Hanne Laceulle (2018) calls for "narratives of becoming" containing "both the potential for growth and
flourishing that later life harbours, and its radicalized confrontation
with existential vulnerability" (258). Put another way, declining physical
health or increased dependence on others does not preclude self-realization. Laceulle builds upon the work of cultural gerontologists such as
Gullette (2004) and Cruikshank (2013), who have argued for the socially
constructed nature of ageing, but focuses on reframing the ideal of self-
realization to offer a meaning-generating cultural narrative on later life
(Laceulle 2018, 126).

    To at least some fans in the community I studied, *Star Trek: Picard*
functions as an example of a narrative of becoming. The depiction of ageing was even framed as continuing an established *Star Trek*-ethos of in-
clusivity and being ahead of its time: "Brilliantly written, as ever *Star Trek*
explored one more thing, boldly going where no one has dared to go before, a heroic captain ageing on mainstream TV and an amazing actor

daring to touch vulnerability with such grace in front of us all." (Sara, 6 December 2021) Season two sends an arguably even stronger message that one is never too old to change, as Picard confronts childhood trauma and opens himself up to a romantic relationship. In this aspect, *Picard* aligns more closely with Laceulle's (2018) desire for representations of continuing development than with those fans who focused on continuity and defying age. Instead of "self-realization as a process of becoming the best that is in you" (Laceulle 2018, 254), some members of the fan group articulated self-acceptance as staying true to yourself. This suggests an idea of an unchanging true and authentic self, which Laceulle does not subscribe to (2018, 213). Her deconstruction of essentialist authenticity and concept of the narratives of becoming is echoed by Mr. Picard, who emphasised repeatedly, that he viewed Sir Patrick Stewart and the character of Jean-Luc Picard as subject to change and welcomed these changes:

> So I've seen Sir Patrick change as an actor and as a person (that's why I can understand perfectly why Jean-Luc has changed as well, but many fans who don't know Sir Patrick like I do have problems with this). He himself said that with age he's becoming more and more relaxed and is trying out more and more what he could never try out as a teenager. He's more open about his feelings (he likes to kiss Sir Ian McKellen and other men often), he's more open about roles he probably wouldn't have taken back then, and he values doing things and playing characters he's never played before. Variety is the big buzzword of his career. So he's getting richer in experiences, impressions, etc. as he ages. (Mr. Picard, 18 August 2021)

To Mr. Picard, change throughout an actor's lifespan is not a problematic breach of authenticity, but a positive development. I would argue that the text of the show supports self-acceptance entwined with accepting change as well, as the first season culminates in Picard being reborn into a synthetic android body – but a body which looks exactly like his aged human body did up to that point, a body that is programmed to die after living a usual human life span. Despite its commentary on the challenges of ageing, *Star Trek: Picard* ends its first season not by 'cleaning up' its protagonist's age as though it were a problem, but by keeping it on board as an integral part of him. It would be naïve to ignore practical production reasons for this writing choice, but in-universe the choice remains salient: Picard could have been given any synthetic body, and yet he is given a body resembling his 'old' self as closely as possible. Continuing this thread, season two presents Picard as perhaps more vulnerable than ever, by showing him as a frightened child as well as the old man shaped by the traumatic events of childhood. However, the season concludes with Picard choosing not to alter his past and thereby his personality, instead accepting it and forgiving his younger self. In doing so he is "unshackled from the past" ("Farewell", 2.10) and is free to become, as Laceulle would say, "the best that is in him".

Achieving Equilibrium

Star Trek: Picard ultimately refuses to settle on the side of age-as-decline or age-defiance. The series instead presents Jean-Luc Picard as both "the Captain they remember" and a changed man – a continually changing old man – which may help us to understand the wide variety of reactions from fans. This article has revealed that even a comparatively small online group of fans is not a homogeneous collective. Fandom is not purely worshipful, but can encompass disappointment, wistfulness, and conflict. Additionally, the responses from this Facebook group have demonstrated that negative opinions do not simply stem from a generalised dislike of aged celebrities or of contemporary storytelling, but more specifically from a perceived breach in continuity. To a portion of audience members, *Star Trek: Picard* successfully integrates change and vulnerability into the ageing casts' stories. Others hold the opinion that the series fails to tell a story that is coherent to what came before and fails to stay true to the spirit of the characters and narrative universe.

As gendered double standards continue to shape the experience of ageing, advances in anti-ageing technologies have the potential to increase pressure on women to defy age. How the experiences of fans and creators are shaped by sexism and intersectional discrimination in fandom spaces, such as the widespread use of objectifying language briefly touched upon here, deserves further study.

In conclusion, while commenters seem to view ageing as a transformation with many negative consequences, they nevertheless hold hope that ageing can be weathered well. This transformation was not conceptualized as inevitably affecting everyone the same way, but as a tricky process that must be successfully managed. The meaning of ageing well thus emerged as achieving an equilibrium between staying true to yourself, taking charge of the aspects of ageing which are in your own power, and accepting those vulnerabilities which we must all inevitably face, whether we live in the twenty-first century or at the dawn of the twenty-fifth.

References

"Farewell", 2.10

"Maps and Legends", 1.2

"Remembrance", 1.1

"The Deadly Years", 2.1.

Advantageous. Dir. Jennifer Phang. Netflix, 2015.

Calasanti, Toni, and Neal King. "Intersectionality and age." *Routledge Handbook of Cultural Gerontology*. Eds. Julia Twigg and Wendy Martin. New York and Oxon: Routledge, 2015. 193–200.

Calasanti, Toni. "Combating Ageism: How Successful Is Successful Aging?" *The Gerontologist* 56.6 (2016): 1093–1101.

Cruikshank, Margaret. *Learning to be Old: Gender, Culture, and Aging*. 3rd Edition. Lanham/Boulder/New York/Toronto/Plymouth: Rowman & Littlefield, 2013.

Facebook. *Star Trek: Picard*. https://www.facebook.com/groups/Picardfans/about, 2022

Gullette, Margaret Morganroth. *Aged by Culture*. Chicago: University of Chicago Press, 2004.

Hills, Matt. "Cult TV Revival: Generational Seriality, Recap Culture, and the 'Brand Gap' of Twin Peaks: The Return." *Television & New Media* 19.4 (2018): 310–327.

Hine, Christine. "From Virtual Ethnography to the embedded, embodied, everyday internet." *The Routledge Companion to Digital Ethnography*. Eds. Larissa Hjorth, Heather Horst, Anne Galloway, and Genevieve Bell. London: Routledge, 2016. 21–28.

Hurd Clarke, Laura, and Erica V. Bennett. "Gender, ageing and appearance." *Routledge Handbook of Cultural Gerontology*. Eds. Julia Twigg and Wendy Martin. New York and Oxon: Routledge, 2015. 133–139.

Jenkins, Henry. "Introduction. Confessions of an Aca/Fan." Jenkins, Henry. *Fans, Bloggers, and Gamers: Exploring Participatory Culture*. New York: New York University Press, 2006. 1–6.

Jones, Bethan. "'Are you ready for this?' 'I don't know if there's a choice'. Cult Reboots, The X-Files Revival, and Fannish Expectations." *The Routledge Companion to Media Fandom*. Eds. Melissa A. Click and Suzanne Scott. New York: Routledge, 2017. 347–355.

Jones, Norma, and Bob Batchelor. "Introduction. Bad Abides: Jeff Bridges, Ideal Aging Hero." *Aging Heroes. Growing Old in Popular Culture*. Eds. Bob Batchelor and Norma Jones. Lanham/Boulder/New York/London: Rowman & Littlefield, 2015. xi–xx.

Katz, Stephen, and Toni Calasanti. "Critical Perspectives on Successful Aging: Does It 'Appeal More Than It Illuminates'?" *The Gerontologist* 55.1 (2015): 26–33.

Laceulle, Hanne. *Aging and Self-Realization. Cultural Narratives about Later Life*. Bielefeld: transcript, 2018.

Lovett, Jamie. "Star Trek: Digital De-Aging Tech Helped Convince Brent Spiner to Return as Data in Picard". *Comicbook*, 21 January 2020. https://comicbook.com/startrek/news/star-trek-picard-data -return-brent-spiner-cgi-de-aging/

Memory Alpha. *IDIC*. https://memory-alpha.fandom.com/wiki/IDIC

r/startrekpicard. https://www.reddit.com/r/startrekpicard/.

Radway, Janice. "Interpretive Communities and Variable Literacies: The Functions of Romance Reading." *Daedalus* 113.3 (1984): 49–73.

Rowe, John W., and Robert L. Kahn. "Successful Aging." *The Gerontologist* 37.4 (1997): 433–440.

Sirtis, Marina, and Brent Spiner. Interview by Ken Reilly. "Marina Sirtis and Brent Spiner on Returning for STAR TREK: PICARD, Digital De-Aging, and Stolen Wigs". *Trekcore*, 13 January 2020. http://blog.trekcore.com/2020/01/interview-marina-sirtis-brent-spiner-returning-star-trek-picard/.

Sontag, Susan. "The double standard of ageing." *The Saturday Review* 23 September 1972: 29–38. Print.

Spruck Wrigley, Sylvia. "Age and Aging." *The Routledge Handbook of Star Trek*. Eds. Leimar Garcia-Siino, Sabrina Mittermeier, and Stefan Rabitsch. New York: Routledge, 2022. 421–429.

Star Trek: Picard. Created by Akiva Goldsman, Michael Chabon, Kirsten Beyer, and Alex Kurtzman, CBS All Access, 2020–2022.

Star Trek: The Original Series. Created by Gene Roddenberry, NBC 1966–1969.

Gender, Rage, and Age in Alanis Morissette's "Reasons I Drink"

Karen Fournier

Abstract: *Alanis Morissette's recent single, "Reasons I Drink" (2019), provides a powerful critique of the erasure of middle-aged females in rock. In this song, the singer-songwriter recounts how she has found peace in middle-age by coming to terms with various negative behaviours that shaped her youth. In the video, she strips away the mythologies surrounding female youth in a narrative that is populated by troubled characters who represent younger incarnations of herself. These characters gather at a therapy session led by the middle-aged artist, in the role of the therapist/sage. This paper will examine the song and video through the lens of Helene Moglen's 2008 feminist concept of "transaging" – a concept that nods towards queer theory to describe the dysphoria that can exist between a woman's perception of her age (driven by memories of youth) and society's perception of the aging female body (driven by a woman's embodied appearance). According to Moglen's theory, the middle-aged self is an amalgam of the various self-states experienced by women at different points their lives. Moglen suggests that women can remain relevant in a culture that privileges youth by shifting focus away from futile attempts to recreate youth and towards critical reflections on the ways in which youthful states have contributed to middle-age identities. Themes explored in Morissette's song and video therefore provide productive and fruitful avenues for other ageing women to explore in popular culture, and the commercial success of this recent song demonstrates that there is a market of women for whom this narrative will resonate.*

Keywords: *Alanis Morissette; popular music; gender; female rage; ageism; Helene Moglen; transaging*

Introduction

After an eight-year hiatus from the recording studio, Alanis Morissette released her ninth studio album, *Such Pretty Forks in the Road*, on July 31, 2020, marking almost exactly 25 years since the release of her break-through album, *Jagged Little Pill*, on June 13, 1995. In the earlier album, Morissette's frank and uncensored depictions of female coming-of-age angst propelled her to fame at the age of twenty-one and prompted some in the popular music press to characterize her as the archetypal 'angry young woman'. This description has also informed scholarly studies of her early work. Kristen Schilt, for example, notes that "anger, which had hitherto been male territory, had a very female voice in Morissette's lyrics" and she argues that, by 1995, Morissette "was suddenly being hailed as a new feminist heroine" because she modelled public displays of rage to other women (Schilt 2003, 10–11). This reading of Morissette's work has become a yardstick against which her entire oeuvre has been measured and, in some cases, unfairly criticized in the popular press. Reviews of her recent studio album provide examples. The *New Musical Express (NME)*, for example, notes that although her latest work, *Such Pretty Forks in the Road* "might not fizz with exactly the same visceral anger as on that seminal record, [...] there's still an urgency and rawness to Morissette" (Daly 2020), while a review in *The Guardian* laments the fact that "there is nothing as thrillingly angry as [the 1995 single] 'You Oughta Know' on the artist's newest album" (Mongredien 2020). A review in *Pitchfork* is similarly lukewarm when it describes the album as "vulnerable, sedate, [and] ballad-heavy" and claims that "most of those ballads are unobtrusive" – in other words, that the album seems low-key (St. Asaph 2020). A *Rolling Stone* critic credits ageing for the perceptions of Morissette's more muted expressions of emotion when he writes that she "became an overnight superstar because she was jilted and angry and she thought the world ought to know [... but] now that she's older, she seems to have reconciled some of her demons and the embers of her angst have been replaced by generalized anxiety and depression" (Grow 2020).

By centering "anger" in their reviews of Morissette's recent album (through its alleged absence in comparison to her early work), music critics continue to respond to, and reinforce, gender norms surrounding public displays of anger by women. In her study of the sexism faced by women in American politics, Rebecca Traister has argued that an angry woman is typically understood as "a perversion of both nature and social norms. She is ugly, emotional, out of control, sick, unhappy, unpleasant to be around, unpersuasive, irrational, crazy, infantile. Above all, she must not be heard" (Traister 2018, 51). Traister's comments arise from her observations of such public figures as Hillary Clinton, Nancy Pelosi, Kamala Harris, and Michelle Obama, and she argues that, to have a successful career, a woman must suppress her anger. She notes that women who occupy multiple sites of oppression (whose identities reside at the intersections of race, gender, and age, for example) are subjected to greater policing of their rage because its expression will transgress both gender norms and social expectations surrounding race and/or age. The same holds true in popular music, where male anger and aggression is so permissible and pervasive that it rarely calls the attention of the popular press. Schilt notes that rock is redolent with expressions of male anger against ex-lovers, but she argues that what made Morissette unique in 1995 was that she exposed how women might feel about betrayals in their personal relationships. Rock's aggression is coded as male, so when a woman who is admitted into rock's sphere engages in anger, she must be called out (Schilt 2003, 13). I contend that anger has been weaponized by critics against Morissette, as it has been against female politicians and public figures, to diminish her potential role as a 'new feminist heroine' for middle-aged and older female fans who find few representations in the popular press. Her fame, and the potential it provides to reach other older women who 'must not be heard', makes Morissette a target for the press, where her age is used to silence the anger that she expresses in her latest album – an anger that reflects her experiences as a middle-aged woman who muses on her long and challenging career in the music industry.

The following analysis will expose how the intersection of sexism and ageism informs critical denials of 'rage' in Morissette's current work, and how she has responded in this work. I will argue that Morissette's latest album, *Such Pretty Forks in the Road*, marks the latest stage in a personal journey that has propelled Morissette through various life-choices and turning-points, as its title suggests. Like all her work, the album engages in many topics across its various tracks, but I will focus on the lead single, "Reasons I Drink," because it deals most explicitly with the topics of ageing and female rage. I will divide my analysis into two parts to tackle how these two themes are represented in the song and to offer thoughts about how Morissette resists conventions of gender and ageing in this song. In the first part of this chapter, I will appeal to feminist theory and social psychology to reclaim the rage that is denied to Morissette by critics of her latest album and to illustrate how Morissette expresses rage in "Reasons I Drink." The analysis will begin with a close reading of the song's lyrics, their vocal performance, and the music that supports both. This portion of the analysis will demonstrate how Morissette becomes what Simon Frith would describe as the protagonist of the song who is "controlling the plot, with an attitude of tone and voice" and how that mixes with "the character of the singer as star, what we know about them or are led to believe about them through their packaging and publicity." (Frith 1996, 198–199). While the anger that I perceive in this song draws a direct line back to her earlier work and therefore serves as another example of female rage, the topic of ageing is not an explicit feature of this song. Instead, ageing is foregrounded in the music video, whose protagonist is the middle-aged Morissette. Carol Vernallis notes that "the music-video image [...] attempts to pull us in with a sense of experience as internally felt rather than externally understood" (Vernallis 2004, 177). In the case of "Reasons I Drink," the harm that results from the youthful behaviours recounted in the song's lyrics become inscribed on Morissette's body and draw the ageing female listener into a shared narrative about the price that we pay for our youthful excesses. My analysis of the video will focus on the interrelationship of lyrics, music, and image to show how the song comes to challenge the conventional binary framework of ageing, where the male gaze that dominates the music industry within which Morissette has built her career is complicit in separating desirable young women from their older, unwanted counterparts. Using Helene Moglen's theory of ageing (outined in the 2008 essay, "Ageing and Transageing: Transgenerational Hauntings of the Self"), I will show how "Reasons I Drink" offers a more liberating representation of female ageing, and one that continues to afford women access to a breadth of emotional expressions, including the rage for which older women are particularly sanctioned.

Reclaiming Female Rage in the Song "Reasons I Drink"

In a recent *Guardian* interview, Morissette explained that "Reasons I Drink" was written to reflect her experiences of "work addiction, love addiction, and food addiction", each of which she has used to cope with the pressures of fame and her experiences in the music industry (Barlow 2020). The song narrates the inner turmoil experienced by a female protagonist who attempts to reconcile the perils of addiction with the benefits and comfort that they provide at challenging times in her life. Musically, this turmoil is expressed in stark contrasts between intimate, confessional verses and strident, defiant choruses. Its two verses are constructed as statements of cause-and-effect, where the opening lines describe a suppressed emotion (for example, in the first verse: "I tell everyone I'm fine even though I am not") while the closing lines show how that repression is channeled into various kinds of addictive behaviours (for example, "I've been working [...] since I was single digits"). Morissette performs each verse in the lower register of her chest voice, which give the verses a sense of intimacy as she discloses each addiction and its source in her life. She is accompanied by a sparse piano vamp, or repeated rhythmic figure, during the verse, allowing the listener to focus on the singer's confessional without the distraction of competing musical parts. Morissette explains that this section of the song is meant to reveal a "very deep, profound sadness and vulnerability" or a melancholy about certain experiences or events in her life (online interview in *Pitchfork*, September 2020). In the second verse, for example, the singer lashes out at a "sick [music] industry" that Morissette has openly faulted for the abuse that she has endured through a career marked by overwork, predatory recording contracts, body shaming, sexual assault, and, most recently, the theft of $5 million by her business manager, Jonathan Schwartz, who was charged with embezzlement in 2017.

As the song moves through the pre-chorus and into the chorus, Morissette shifts to her upper vocal register, which highlights her narrator's growing anxiety and ambivalence as she ponders the daunting prospect of facing life's challenges without the support of her various emotional crutches. She testifies that "nothing can give reprieve like they [i.e., her addictions] do," and the physical exertion required to sing this line in her head voice echoes and reinforces the mounting tension in the song. The vocal performance is loudest and most forceful in the chorus, in which the narrator competes for attention in a mix that now comprises the guitar, keyboards, and drumkit. "Here we are!" she announces at the beginning of the chorus, which describes the emotional high that she experiences each time she engages with one of her addictions. The song reaches its melodic climax in the chorus on the words "rapture" and "helpful," to suggest that the singer is disinclined to abandon the short-term benefits afforded by her addictions despite the long-term damage they inflict on her physical and emotional well-being. As the chorus concludes, the lyrics unravel into a series of vowel sounds that become embedded into the instrumental mix. At this point in the song, the narrator appears to have escaped into an altered state of consciousness, consistent with the "high" that she describes in each verse. However, the voice quickly descends during this musical passage and returns to the original lower register in preparation for the reappearance of the verse. In each case, the vocal line descends in register to suggest that the singer's high is fleeting and that it is inevitably interrupted by the "profound sadness" of the narrator's reality. At the end of the song, the listener remains unsure about its outcome: does this narrator manage to kick her addictions, or does the song merely serve to point out how the stress of modern life often prompts people to seek escapist pleasures that can never be fully abandoned?

Because it tells a tale of personal challenges and the negative behavioural responses that they engender, "Reasons I Drink" might seem to foreground depression more than anger (consistent with critic's observations about the seeming lack, or tempering, of anger in her recent work). I would argue however, that these two emotions are often closely aligned, and that repressed rage can manifest as depression (among other things). Causal links between internalized anger and depression in women have been theorized most famously by Freud (1917), whose essentialized reading of gender has since been contested, but whose interpretation of depression as repressed rage has been adapted to studies of female rage by feminists and social psychologists. Judith Butler (1995) has suggested that subordination by gender and sexuality creates what she describes as a "melancholy" that serves as the public face of an internalized anger experienced by oppressed subjects whose behaviours are socially prescribed and circumscribed. Butler builds on Freud's definition of melancholy as "the unfinished process of grieving [...] in which [a] lost object is incorporated and phantasmatically preserved in and as the ego" (Butler 1995, 166). She proposes a gendered reading of melancholia in which women grieve versions of themselves that are denied to them because of social mores that restrict gender expression and regulate gendered behaviours. According to Butler, "in the 'normal' constitution of gender presentation, the gender that is performed is constituted by a set of disavowed attachments [and] identifications that constitute a different domain of the 'unperformable'" (Butler 1995, 177). In this gendered reframing of "melancholy," Butler argues that women internalize and grieve unperformable aspects of themselves (like anger, which is strongly coded as male). Denied emotional expressions become supplanted by passive emotional expressions coded as female. Through this interpretive lens, the "deep, profound sadness" described by Morissette as central to "Reasons I Drink" can be understood as melancholy, or as the grief that she experiences for her repressed anger. On its surface, "Reasons I Drink" seems antithetical to Morissette's more famous song, "You Oughta Know", which is infused with anger, but I would argue that the current song is a paean to the angry young woman who has been preserved in the singer's ego, but whose anger has been repressed.

The song's verses present the female listener with plenty to identify with and rage against, but the rage simmers in these sections of the song, and in place of an explosive release in the chorus, the narrative turns towards a description of how rage might be channeled elsewhere. A 2008 study of career women by two emotion theorists classifies rage as a "status emotion" available to dominant members of society (that is, white males) and denied to those whose identities mark them as subordinate. Data within this study leads its authors to conclude that, while white male anger tends to be perceived as a normal and objective response to adverse external circumstances, "the derogated status of angry women appeared to be due to the degree to which their behavior was seen as internally motivated – in particular, to the perception that they were out of control" (Brescoll and Uhlmann 2008, 273). Women who display anger at an external incident or occurrence that warrants their rage transgress the lower status that they inhabit relative to their white male counterparts, who can engage freely in their rage. The response to this transgression of status is to pathologize female rage, which will manifest in other ways. The tendency for women to redirect their anger, often into self-destructive behaviours, is well documented by social psychologists who examine the personal costs of repressed female rage. A 2013 study of anger expression in a sample of 239 white female subjects reveals that, while male rage is socially accepted, "women suffer anger in silence, or maladaptively divert it to indirect means of expression which become transformed into other pathologies such as bulimia, self-cutting, and substance abuse, or health problems such as hypertension, coronary heart disease, or obesity" (González-Prendes, Praill, and Kernsmith 2013, 122). In response to repressed female rage or melancholy "Reasons I Drink" illustrates how that rage can be redirected through reference to the pathologies of alcoholism, in the title and first verse, and overeating, in the second verse. While these two emotional substitutes are referenced directly in the song, "Reasons I Drink" also suggests that female anger can be stifled by other harmful activities that are described in the lyrics, notable among which include overwork and overspending.

"Reasons I Drink" can be interpreted as a song about the self-harm that arises in response to inhibitions placed on female expressions of rage. It opens a window onto the social norms that stifle the 'angry young woman' who burst on the scene in 1995 and, following Butler, it explains how women might grieve their anger by redirecting repressed rage into the addictive behaviours described in the lyrics. While the narrator might list several reasons to drink, primary among them is the one reason that remains unstated in the song: namely, the melancholy felt by someone who must suppress a pathologized female anger or risk infantilization by a society that derides female rage. As the song reveals, this melancholy emerges as a set of addictions that enable the protagonist to grieve her angry younger self. Fans know that Morissette is middle aged, but the song neither references her age nor requires a middle-aged performer to make the song meaningful. Access to the "status emotion" of rage, as described by Brescoll and Uhlmann (2008), is denied to women of *all* ages, which means that the song could be performed convincingly by a woman in her teens or twenties, especially when we consider the prevalence of self-harming and addictive behaviours among younger women. One purpose of my recuperation of Morissette's rage has been to challenge critical misrepresentations of her current work and to assert that rage continues to infuse some of her songs. Another purpose will be to consider how the theme of repressed rage might align with the representation of age and ageing in the song's music video, where visual references to youth coexist and interact with references to Morissette's ageing self, and where the repressed anger of the song's lyrics and Morissette's performance can be read both as sexist and ageist.

Representing Female Ageing in the Video "Reasons I Drink"

While "Reasons I Drink" is non-specific in its representation of female age, the music video centers the topics of gender, age, and ageing, and their potential intersection with rage. In watching the video for the first time, I was struck at how much it echoed the positive and creative performance of ageing that was proposed by the literary theorist Helene Moglen in her 2008 essay, "Ageing and Transageing: Transgenerational Hauntings of the Self". Drawing upon her own experience of ageing, and one that resonates with me, Moglen observes that, despite the corporeal reality of her present, past selves remain available to her through youthful memories of herself. After one notable encounter with her own ageing image in the mirror, she concludes that "in our reflections, [ageing subjects] glimpse the familiar self we have prepared ourselves to see and a shadow self that is alien and unknown" (Moglen 2008a, 298). Moglen proposes that a conventional conception of ageing as a chronological experience separating younger and older selves only gives us a fraction of the story about the actual experience of ageing – and, she notes, perceptions of age as points on a historical continuum merely reinforce the diminishing privileges afforded to us as we move through time. From her own experience, she contends that the experience of ageing is actually more nuanced, and she argues for a description of ageing, rooted in psychoanalytic theory, that emerges from relationships between various self-states drawn asynchronously from across the lifespan of the ageing subject. One's present identity is understood in Moglen's theory as an amalgam of past identities which are stored in, and recuperated from, the psyche (2008a). But unlike the subject whose sense of self, or "ideal ego," is born at the moment that they gaze upon themselves for the first time in Lacan's mirror, the ageing subject in Moglen's mirror glimpses a corporeal self that she must reconcile with her memories of past self-states that she views in in her mind's eye. As Moglen's subject ages, her identity becomes moored by traces of past selves that are reflected on the surface of her ageing face, each of which provides an interpretative framework for the otherwise alien aspects of that ageing image: put differently, certain aspects of the ageing face bear the traces of their origins in the past while others cue the reality of the present. The process of ageing is therefore marked in Moglen's theory by an initial sense of alienation from the ageing self and its eventual incorporation into the psyche as a modified version of the past (Moglen 2008a). The cycle of alienation and incorporation repeats across the lifetime of the subject as she seeks to interpret each new ageing self-image. The ageing subject therefore becomes richer, not diminished, over time as she fuses older experiences with those in the present. Moglen (2008a) uses the term "transageing" to describe this process not only because it resists the rigid states of 'young' and 'old' that mark the conventional age binary (and therefore proposes a spectrum of ageing identities), but also because it posits that transgenerational self-states work together to create the ageing self across permeable boundaries that are transitional, or that shift and change as we move through time. In this reconceptualization of ageing, the subject reclaims the agency to determine possibilities for her ageing self, and her performance of ageing will be guided by unique memories of past experiences of her younger selves that are preserved for posterity in her psyche.

"Reasons I Drink" provides an example of the mirror at work. Directed by the Los Angeles filmmaker Erin Elders and released on 27 February 2020, the video introduces Morissette as a facilitator who interacts with younger versions of herself at an Alcoholics Anonymous (AA) meeting. Before the music begins, the singer walks towards a large folding table in a non-descript church hall, pours herself a cup of coffee from a large urn, and joins the group that awaits her in the center of the room. The blazer that she wears signals her status as the meeting's facilitator while her reading glasses suggest that she is a middle-aged woman. As the song unfolds, the viewer is introduced to other members of the meeting, among which include three younger versions of the singer, each played by Morissette dressed in an outfit that points to a particular time in her life. One of these versions appears in an oversized white shirt and dark eye make-up, recalling the 21-year-old version of the singer who appeared in the video of her breakout song, "You Oughta Know". Consistent with the fame lavished on Morissette after the release of this song, this version of the singer is primped by make-up artists, pursued by a music executive who implores her to sign a contract, pestered by fans for her autograph, and interviewed on television. Another variant of Morissette, from the same era in the singer's life, wears a red knit cap and multi-coloured winter scarf that recalls her appearance in the video "Ironic". She rebuffs a priest who moves his chair beside her to offer a comforting hand and turns away from a reporter who approaches her for an interview. Through these actions Morissette hints at unwanted intrusions of the press into her life and also reveals her conflicted relationship to Catholicism, which she describes another the song from the same period, "Forgiven", from her first album. A third, and older, version of Morissette appears in the guise of a disheveled new mother in her thirties who, like the real-life singer, appears to struggle with post-partum depression away from the public eye. She nurses a baby who is whisked away by a nurse and later appears with two older children. Each of Morissette's youthful iterations links a particular time in her life with a specific addiction chronicled in the song. She drinks and is medicated because of the challenges of motherhood and, as the video shows, because she is expected to leave her children reluctantly in the care of a nanny when the demands of motherhood clash with the demands of her career. She works obsessively as a 21-year-old with a thirst for fame but discovers that she can never satisfy the demands of the music industry, so she seeks validation in overspending and overeating.

The first two thirds of the video tells the story of a conventional AA session, but as the narrator performs the bridge and the final chorus, the session goes awry. The camera pans across Morissette's three youthful selves and we find them engaged in various scenes of mayhem. One version of the 21-year-old Morissette is pursued by a trio of fans while the 30-something mother attempts to break up a fight between her two older children. The pages of the recording contract that a young Morissette signed earlier in the video are tossed about as the middle-aged Morissette, in her role as the counsellor, stands and surveys the havoc from the center of the room. Sara Ahmed (2017) explains how ageing, and the accumulation of lived experience, teaches women to suppress their rage and how this suppression can trigger a cathartic response like the one depicted at this turning-point in the video. Ahmed notes that

> it is from difficult experiences, of being bruised by structures that are not even revealed to others, that [women] gain the energy to rebel.

It is from what we come up against that we gain new angles on what we are against. Our bodies become our tools; our rage becomes sickness [and as we age,] we begin to feel the weight of histories more and more; the more we expose the weight of history, the heavier it becomes. We snap. We snap under the weight; things break (Ahmed 2017, 255).

The climactic scene in "Reasons I Drink" is one of chaos and catharsis, or a release of the pent-up rage that lies behind the addictions described in the song's lyrics. But, curiously, these expressions of rage are observed by the middle-aged facilitator who opts against participating in them. She walks unscathed through the mayhem as if she is in dream. By contrast, her youthful self-states are troubled and unsettled: they are the ones who list their pathological responses to the societal pressures they face and who ultimately snap. They turn to the middle-aged Morissette for the advice that her life experience might bring. Her appearance in the video is calming and she provides an assurance to these transgenerational selves that they will survive their youthful troubles to find the emotional stability that she has found in middle age. In its representations of female youth as despondent and self-doubting and of middle age as stable and secure, "Reasons I Drink" therefore upends conventional messaging about female ageing that foregrounds youth as the ideal variant of the female self. Instead, it tells a more liberating kind of story about female ageing that prompts a reassessment of the stereotypes and exclusions implicit in ageist dismissals of women.

"Reasons I Drink" also gives us an example of how female ageing might cue empowerment through the empathy can arise from identification with others. The video is framed by scenes that signify Morissette's existence as a middle-aged woman in the present: her appearance starts the narrative and her exit concludes it. This is the version of Morissette that is 'real' in comparison to the imagined versions of her younger self who emerge and interact in the middle of the story. As noted, these versions narrate various life challenges, as if to entertain 'what if' questions about choices made by the narrator's younger selves as they stood at various forks in the road during her life. One youthful ghost seems to raise the question about how her career might have taken a different path if she had known better than to sign a predatory recording contract. Another speculates on how her mental health might have been spared if she had defiantly shunned the media during the height of her fame. The third ponders the negative impact of her career on her capacity to serve as a mother to her children as they are taken away by a caregiver or as they fight for her limited attention. If we read their presence in the video through Moglen's metaphor of the mirror, these characters represent younger variants of the singer who present themselves as memories etched on the face of the present (the concept of the mirror is described in Moglen 2008a and 2008b). They remain available to Morissette through her recollections of their actions and the feelings of helplessness, hopelessness, and – importantly – rage that these actions engendered in the past. But it is also significant that these self-states are imagined, unreal, disembodied, and ghosts. By the end of the video, we discover (alongside Morissette) that the events portrayed in the AA meeting and the characters engaged in the video's narrative exist solely in her mind. As we return to the therapy circle after the climax of the narrative, we can see that Morissette's momentary daydream was triggered by similarities that she perceived between her younger self-states and women in the therapy circle. These shared identity markers prompt recollections of past self-states, and these recollections fuel the empathy that Morissette's facilitator feels for those who suffer. This empathy – a product of years of life experience – makes Morissette the 'good' therapist that we assume her to be in this story.

Finally, it is also important to recognize the broader implications of the disassociation of ageing from the body in this narrative. While it might be true that the middle-aged Morissette is actually *more* corporeal in this narrative than her ethereal psychic ghosts, their presence in the narrative shifts the locus of ageing to the mind, where Morissette can construct different versions of herself from remembered self-stages – versions that assist in her empathy for the other characters who appear alongside her in the video. This aspect of the video illustrates one of the central contributions of Moglen's theory (outlined in 2008a and elaborated in 2008b): that by engaging, reinterpreting, and assimilating the wide array of "who we used be" as we age, we can replace the script that tells women to feel shame about the disintegration of their bodies with a script that celebrates the ageing woman as a vibrant, multi-layered being deserving of attention for the various experiences that she has endured and that she can share (Moglen 2008a).

Intersections of Age and Rage in "Reasons I Drink"

I began this chapter with the assertion that 'anger' was an oversimpli-fication of Morissette's early work, which exhibits an emotional depth that resists a single label. At the same time, the omnipresence of 'rage' as a marker in descriptions of Morissette's early music makes its alleged absence in critiques of her current work noteworthy. My analysis of the lyrics and aspects of their performance demonstrates that rage lies be-hind the various addictions enumerated in her recent song, "Reasons I Drink". I would like to conclude with some observations about how that rage informs the video and, specifically, how it intersects with gender and age in the visual narrative.

Writing for *Rolling Stone* in 2020, Kory Grow argues that Morissette's rage has been tempered by her ageing, and that she has reconciled some of the "demons" with which she struggled in her youth. The video "Reasons I Drink" challenges this assessment, however, as Morissette continues to project her rage through the memories embodied and performed by her youthful selves. The reading offered here invites us to consider Moglen's view of ageing, which defines ageing as an ongoing process informed by what she describes as prior "self-states". In partic-ular, Moglen's theory of age and ageing can be used to explain the video's final moments, when Morissette appears to awaken from a daydream that had been populated by her raging younger selves (Moglen 2008a and 2008b).

As the video draws to its conclusion, Morissette stands in the mid-dle of the room with her coffee cup in hand and, as the mayhem van-ishes in an instant, she faces a group of strangers who encircle her. Three are dressed in clothing that trigger youthful associations in Morissette's mind, but these three women are not phantoms from her past. They are strangers. The confusion written across their faces implies that they have witnessed the release of rage that Morissette imagined for the youthful selves in her dream. As with the fractured self-image that appears in Moglen's mirror, this youthful rage remains recognizable in the ageing face that meets the shocked gaze of the AA meeting's participants. Morissette's youthful anger remains evident on her face as an "image of the past" that continues to inform the older version of Morissette whose psyche drives this narrative. The message in the video thereby complements the message in the song: that women of all ages rage, but that female rage (which is taboo for women of all ages) must be increasing repressed as women age. As the reactions to Morissette's rage illustrate at the end of the video, the need to repress rage is particularly true of older women who engage with that "status emotion" and who thereby risk losing the authority that they might have accrued over the course of their careers (Brescoll and Ihlmann, 2008). I would argue that the title of Morissette's recent album and lead single both point to rage as an emotion that lurks within the female psyche and whose repression leads to other kinds of behaviours. Morissette looks back at the various dilemmas, or "forks in the road", that she faced over the course of her career, and many of these are performed in "Reasons I Drink". In looking back at younger iterations of herself, Morissette recognizes the anger that she felt at moments when she was exploited by the music industry or stripped of any power to make her own decisions. As a woman, she is denied the status emotion of rage, the repression of which she diverts into other kinds of behaviours that continue to have their impact on the 'real' Morissette who appears as the facilitator in the video. To suggest that rage is absent from her current work is to reinforce a binary model of female ageing in which older women are reduced to silent shells of their former youthful selves.

While the distinction between 'anger' and the more anodyne descriptions of Morissette's latest album might seem semantic on their surface, I would argue that the terms are used strategically in the popular music press to foreclose on the possibility of the 'angry *older* woman'. And why might that be? Simply, anger draws the kind of attention that would otherwise be denied to an older performer in an industry that privileges female youth and beauty. By denying that Morissette's current work is infused with anger (among other emotions that are equally represented across her extensive body of work), the media reinforces the stereotype of the female artist who should 'age gracefully' into the obscurity afforded by retirement.

References

Ahmed, Sara. *Living a Feminist Life*. Durham: Duke University Press, 2017.

Barlow, Eve. "Alanis Morissette: 'Without Therapy, I Don't Think I'd Still Be Here'." *The Guardian*, 24 July 2020. https://www.theguardian.com/music/2020/jul/24/alanis-morissette-without-therapy-i-dont-think-id-still-be-here

Brescoll, Victoria L. and Eric Luis Ihlmann. "Can an Angry Woman Get Ahead? Status Conferral, Gender, and Expression of Emotion in the Workplace." *Psychological Science* 19.3 (2008): 268–275.

Butler, Judith. "Melancholy Gender – Refused Identification." *Psychoanalytical Dialogues* 5.2 (1995): 165–180.

Daly, Rhian. "Alanis Morissette's 'Reasons I Drink' is another piece of raw, urgent pop from an artist as vital as ever". New Musical Express, 2 December 2020. https://www.nme.com/reviews/alanis-morissette-reasons-i-drink-track-review-2583236

Freud, Sigmund. "Mourning and Melancholia." *Collected Papers* 4. Ed. Ernest Jones (trans. Joan Rivière). New York: Basic Books, 1960 [1917]. 153–170.

Frith, Simon. *Performing Rites: On the Value of Popular Music*. Cambridge: Harvard University Press, 1996.

González-Prendes, A. Antonio, Nancy Praill, and Poco Kernsmith. "Age Differences in Women's Anger Experience and Expression." *International Journal of Psychological Studies* 5.3 (2013): 122–134.

Grow, Kory. "Alanis Morissette Takes the Safe Path on New Album 'Such Pretty Forks in the Road'." *Rolling Stone*, 20 July, 2020. https://www.rollingstone.com/music/music-album-reviews/alanis-morissette-such-pretty-forks-in-the-road-review-1036004/

Moglen, Helene. "Ageing and Transageing: Transgenerational Haunt-ings of the Self." *Studies in Gender and Sexuality* 9.4 (2008a): 297–311.

Moglen, Helene. "Feminism, Transageing, and Ageism: A Response to Segal." *Studies in Gender and Sexuality* 9.4 (2008b): 323–327.

Mongredien, Phil. "Alanis Morissette: Such Pretty Forks in the Road review – Back to the Confessional." *The Guardian*, 2 August 2020. https://www.theguardian.com/music/2020/aug/02/alanis-morissette-such-pretty-forks-in-the-road-review-back-to-the-confessional

Morissette, Alanis. "Reasons I Drink." Epiphany Records, 2019.

Morissette, Alanis. "Reasons I Drink." *YouTube*, https://www.youtube.com/watch?v=jWHpIP1-kUI.

Morissette, Alanis. *Jagged Little Pill*. Maverick Records, 1995.

Morissette, Alanis. *Such Pretty Forks in the Road*. Epiphany Records, 2020.

Pitchfork. "Critical Breakthroughs: Interview with Alanis Morissette. How Alanis Morissette Creates Emotional Vocal Performances." *YouTube*, , https://www.youtube.com/watch?v=Mgut6HTtVhY.

Schilt, Kristen. "'A Little Too Ironic': The Appropriation and Packaging of Riot Grrrl Politics by Mainstream Female Musicians." *Popular Music and Society* 26.1 (2003): 5–16.

St. Asaph, Katherine. "Albums: Such Pretty Forks in the Road," *Pitchfork*, 6 August 2020. https://pitchfork.com/reviews/albums/alanis-morissette-such-pretty-forks-in-the-road/?verso=true.

Traister, Rebecca. *Good and Mad: The Revolutionary Power of Women's Anger*. New York: Simon & Schuster, 2018.

Vernallis, Carol. *Experiencing Music Video: Aesthetics and Cultural Context*. New York: Columbia University Press, 2004.

On Being Silenced and Breaking Cycles
Deliberating Patters of Violence in Tori Amos' Works

Melinda Niehus-Kettler

Abstract: *While her experiencing forms of violence has inspired Tori Amos to write, her works can be conceived of as forms of defiance. She tells us stories about domestic, political, and environmental violence, about rape and miscarriage – as well as matriarchal power. Many of the topics she addresses in her songs and memoirs are tabooed. Perceiving her as lacking the authority to speak up, (self-proclaimed) authorities have repeatedly tried to silence the singer-songwriter. Above all, popular culture and stories told through music trans-/form and become part of our embodied affective makeup, knowledge, and resistance. Pieces of music become pieces of our identities and (hi-)stories. However, whose, what, and when stories are told – or remain untold – depends on social, cultural, and historical frameworks, on the dominant perspective of the authors and authorities. In patriarchal, capitalistic, and (post)colonial systems, patterns of violence and the "economy of credibility" (Fricker 2007, 1) still affect the identities of the others, e.g. those perceived as female and/or past the age of childbearing, much more adversely than the norms, e.g. cisgender and/or siring men. Amos' thematising different form of violence and gender-based discrimination can be conceived of as defying these embodied audio-visual hierarchies and as breaking cycles of abuse. Her breaking her own silence has re-/created relatability and connections among allies. It has fostered interrelationships between her and her audiences, among members of imagined communities who feel represented through her voice and in their shared (hi)stories.*

Keywords: *pop music; lived experience; storytelling; domestic violence; patterns of violence; Otherness; abuse cycles; resistance; epistemic injustice; embodied audio-visual hierarchies*

Introduction – "And Become All That They Told You"[1]

The voice in "Girl" (1992) wonders if perhaps, someday, after being "everybody else's girl," "she will be her own" (Amos 2020, 36). When Tori Amos elaborates on the "birth" of this song she describes "her" as "not just" "[applying to]" "a young woman's story" (2020, 37–38). The singer-song-writer explains that this "Song Being" is relevant to "anyone" "committing" themselves "to stop being the person someone else needs, demands, or seduces them to be or intimidates them into becoming" (Amos 2020, 37–38). And "[w]hether we become 'this me' to deflect conflict or to stave off rejection, we have all morphed into 'the me' someone else wants us to be" (Amos 2020, 37). With this piece of music, Amos (2020) sketches the power dynamics between "masters" and those whom they perceive as "[pets]" (37). These "masters" "know that people can be trained", "[e]ither with praise, shame, the fear of failure, or the fear of being gaslighted" (Amos 2020, 37). In the end, "[t]his kind of relationship" is "not about joint respectful mutual conditions", it is "all about the master's conditions" (Amos 2020, 37). "[T]he technique is a relationship of rewards and punishments," and "there is no unconditional love" (Amos 2020, 37). Amos asserts, "The mantra of 'Girl'" is "become [your] own owner," "[your] own authority" and "home," find your own "way to live what [you] believe" (2020, 37).

With "Girl", Amos does not depict human relationships or hierarchies based on mutual regard and appreciation. She describes and critiques the abuse of power, the abuse of positions of trust. In many of her songs and chapters of her memoir *Resistance* (2020), she delineates what can be read as distinctive elements of patterns of violence (Norfolk City Council 2022). The concepts of *gender* and (forms of) *violence* define

---

1   "Girl" (Amos 2020, 36)

her works time and time again. So, I feel it is worthwhile to deliberate what meanings these representations of violence and gender in popular music re-/create, in other words, what these "stories can tell us about our wider social locations that are at once personal, political, local, and global" (Sheperd 2013, 2).

From a broader perspective, the individuals that Amos calls "masters" in "Girl" can be conceived of as abusive human beings and institutions. These commonly hide behind the facade of the dedicated parent or partner, the benevolent friend, the honourable member of the community, the righteous clergyman or politician, the philanthropic CEO – the morally superior (self-proclaimed) authority. It might be the allegedly ethical teacher, supervisor, or the "white coats" (Amos 2020, 35, 36). A crucial element of patterns of violence is the destruction of the abused person's sense of self, be it as part of what we might regard as epistemic, medical, or sexual violence. It can be perceived as a progressing annihilation and violence de-/forming a person's individuality from the outside and the inside. Generally, individual harmful bonds and the compliance of those who are being abused might be conceptualised as reflected in and as re-/enforced by structural violence. The obedience and conformity are often based on financial dependency, the fear of humiliation and social stigma, but also a lack of bodily autonomy and an eroded sense of self. Amos' song "Girl" can be regarded as reminiscent of and as mirroring these power dynamics in fragments. Within actual and/or perceived states of dependency, such as power imbalances re-/generated by our patriarchal, capitalistic, and (post-)colonial systems, as part of 'gaslighting' manoeuvres, survivors are taught to doubt their bodily experience/s, their agency, and social value (Amos 2020, 37). All the while, they are trained not to trust others, not to speak of the violence and deception. As the abused are being silenced, they silence themselves. And as they lose their sense of self, they become the identities that the abusive individual and/or society need them to be, namely human beings that neither value, nor own themselves (Amos 2020, 37).

Patriarchy, capitalism and (post)colonialism beget, nurture, and manifest in lopsided binary systems, devaluation, and exploitation. These systems feed on segregation and confinements. On the micro, meso and macro level, they thrive on manifold forms of violence. And their organisations derive from the mindsets and dispositions of their parental, corporate, and governmental authorities. Forms of violence, including colonial, economic, political, psychological, emotional, re-productive, and/or physical violence, and all of the inherent processes leave a lasting mark on a person's perceived identity. By the means of triangulation and smear campaigns, abusers and those who side with them – often to benefit on a financial or emotional level – deny the survivors' cognitive and/or bodily abilities. As part of projection, i.e. the attribution of their own feelings and/or attitudes to other peo-ple, an abusive person and/or society might deny the other people's humanness, intelligence, integrity, and credibility. Furthermore, they re-/present alleged lacks thereof in public (Nussbaum 2004, 75, 111, 129, 341; Fricker 2007, 1). Oftentimes, the degradation is facilitated and justified by infantilisation, pathologisation, and criminalisation. These reinforce perceived Otherness that is un-/consciously re-/constructed with discursive practices and categories such as *gender, age, race, class,* and/or *sexual orientation.* The deceptive re-/presentations and one-sided narratives are tantamount to pre-convictions and, at the same time, within cyclic systems, re-victimise those who have been enduring the violence. They are repeatedly subjected to ridicule and/or threats. Such tactics are part of everyday as well as institutional, for instance moral, medical, and legal discourses and practices (Amos 2020, 36, 119, 128). They all re-/generate divisions, the survivors' disrepute and isolation, as well as lacks of knowledge on the diverse manifestations of abuse. Moreover, through the use of physical and psychological confinements, physical force, neglect, the silent treatment – and/or, on a social level, symbolic annihilation – the abused experience their *selves* being repeat-edly devalued and eliminated. These methods also re-/generate lacks of self-/representations, a lack of diverse stories and, thus, a "gap" in "collective hermeneutical resources" (Fricker 2007, 6, 151). *Au fond,* as part of individual violence as well as forms of systemic discrimination, an abusive person as well as abusive institutions divide and sow doubt among the members of their communities who could become allies and question the abuse of power.

There is an intra-personal effect as well, though. Aforementioned forms of violence condition those who are violated to see themselves through the abusers' eyes and from their perspective. This way, our (social) sanctioning measures beget, nurture, and manifest in the survivors' shame, fear, and alienation time and time again. Since these experiences are internalised and embodied, they often become enduring forms of self-judgement, but also self-punishment and dissociation. It seems, in public view, the abused disappear "in a prison behind [their] eyes" (Amos 2020, 49). All of these aspects influence how they confine themselves, how they conceive of their scope, their mental and/or legal power in our societies. In the end, these manoeuvres permanently affect their self-definition, visibility, and self-representations. And while bodily experience/s such as shame and fear seem to be the most affective elements of our (eventually) embodied power structures, they constitute effective elements of abuse cycles as well (Norfolk City Council 2022).

By and large, relationships in-/formed by abuse cycles can be regarded as self-sustaining and self-justifying. Whereas the "masters'" excuses might alternate, abusive people habitually rewrite history. They select, eliminate, and re-/present events, individuals, and groups in ways that suit their current purposes (Amos 2020, 37). They manage to convince the survivors and others that the abuse either never happened, or that it is not as harmful as those who have actually been harmed perceive it. Violators often play the victim and accuse the abused to be guilty of alleged (sexual) provocations, of lying, and/or irrational behaviour. Above all else, what Amos describes as a "technique," i.e. "a relationship of rewards and punishments" (Amos 2020, 37) can be understood as a cyclic system, a pattern of very different but repetitive phases. In phases of relative calm, some violent individuals and/or institutions might appear to have changed. Some oppressors make concessions. They seem protective and caring. They might grant, now and then, (short-lived) privileges. They also apologise to re-/gain trust and reenforce the bond between the abusers and the survivors. Then, however, the tension builds up and another phase of restrictions, cruelty, and escalating conflicts begins. Rarely do violent people's ill-concealed entitlement and contempt for the abused change. Rarely do their manipulation and behaviour patterns change. More importantly, patterns of violence are difficult to discern. Remarkably enough, it is usually the abused breaking their silence and challenging the abusers' conduct that is perceived as causing disruptions and harm. In a general sense, it is the reaction to the violence that is represented as problematic – not the violence itself.

Not only since the phenomenon of the *#metoo* movement, we must assume that an entertainment and music industry dominated by male authorities, by men focusing on the (young) male gaze and address, re-/generates aforementioned power imbalances and silences. On another level, popular music, song lyrics, and music videos constitute highly effective elements of our power structures as well. They feature and can contribute to our (personal) embodied (hi)stories. Within cyclic systems, the music industry and pop songs incorporate and circulate narratives that re-/generate and normalise, e.g., epistemic and physical violence. Within cycles of profit, they perpetuate and vivify colonial and sexual violence. Thereby, as elements of our patriarchal, capitalist, and (post)colonial systems, they have contributed to systemic discrimination. On an interpersonal and an intra-personal level, they re-/produce systemic violence, i.e. violence that affects our bodies and that is fundamental to our everyday and institutional, e.g. economic, social, and political practices and discourses. All of which appear to re-/form and deform our individual and social bodies. Basically, even (self-proclaimed) authorities in the popular music business, as part of these structures, appear to re-/create and stage the desired stories and desirable bodies.

(Hi)Stories, bodies, and power structures can be reclaimed, though. Becoming aware of the patterns of abusive relationships, we can reclaim the very same elements of our power structures that seem to embrace one-sided stories and fabrics of violence, such as sexism, racism, and ageism. We can use the same social institutions to challenge limited perspectives and those who control our narratives. Many of us have been questioning our (hi)stories and ideals, the re-/enforced invisibility and silence of the identities that our societies seem so anxious to hide and *keep in their place*. By now, there is a growing and impressive body of literature that centres around the "relationship between age, women and popular music" and, thereby, "the achievements of older women in the sphere of popular music" (Jennings and Gardner 2012, 1–2). Numerous works have extensively discussed "the gendered nature of the music industry", the inherent "power dimensions, [the] role and representations of women" (Jennings and Gardner 2012, 2 quto. Whiteley 1997). Moreover, ground-breaking analyses of rather specific performative strategies and relationships between musicians and their fan-bases have illustrated diverse forms of resistance (Jennings and Gardner 2012, 2). Madonna's videos, for example, have been described as "a key site in both the struggle for *self-representation* within the hegemonic space of MTV and an important space for *female identification* within the already overcrowded marketplace for texts that adopt a male adolescent address" (Watson and Railton 2012, 141–142, authors' emphasis). Her perceived transgressions in terms of allegedly gender- and/or age-appropriate behaviour and binary systems such as "male/female, high art/pop art [...], private/public" can be interpreted as forms of resistance to the hegemonic ideals, discourses and social practices encompassed by our power structures (Watson and Railton 2012, 141, citing Kaplan 1987, 126). Other but not dissimilar forms of resistance to stereotypical views and (discursive) practices can be discerned in the works of Tori Amos. Her chosen vulnerability, self-representations, and ongoing processes of self-definition defy the silencing measures from which violent individuals and systems appear to benefit. She empowers her audiences by defying the eliminating processes that, e.g., sexism and ageism re-/enforce.

In my deliberations, Amos' ageing as an element of her perceived identity, her emotional makeup and accumulated knowledge, cannot but must be understood as having affected her embodying and telling of (musical) stories. Her ageing as well as intergenerational experiences, e.g., her daughter's and her mother's (hi)stories are part of her own (hi)story. In this chapter, her ageing, i.e. ageing as a potential factor determining the artist's appearance/s as such will fade into the background, though. I focus on Amos' representations of violence, namely violence that is, more often than not, related to gender and rooted in power imbalances characterising our relationships on a micro, meso, and macro level. It is violence based on and justified by forms of perceived Otherness, i.e. a social construct and potpourri of (bodily) attributes and differences that have a negative connotation. More precisely, my objective is to show how Amos' sharing her experiences with gender-based violence in pop music empowers –- and re-/generates affective connections among – the musician and her audiences. As a rule, in pop music, "many women [...] simply disappear from public view after their moment of fame has passed, leaving behind only an imprint of their youthful selves on the cultural memory" (Watson and Railton 2012, 139). Amos, however, despite a looming and generally widespread age-related invisibility and silence of female artists in the music industry, has spoken up time and time again. She has shed light on forms and patterns of violence. In doing so, she has broken the silence not only for herself, but for and with other generations.

Sharing (Hi)Stories of Violence

"'You survived post-menopause [...]. You need to tell that story so that my future doesn't look like defeat'" (Amos in Marchese 2017). Caring nudges such as this comment by her then-teenage daughter, her own embodied trauma, as well as her mother's losing her voice after a stroke have inspired Tori Amos to use her voice for herself and for others. Hoping that, one day, "more women of more ages" will be heard, she knows that this will only happen if "women's stories of experience" are deemed "something we want to hear," though (Amos in Marchese 2017). The artist's more than fifteen albums and two memoirs comprise stories about ideals of beauty, about rape, miscarriage, environmental and political violence, the boy's club of the music industry, ageing – and matriarchal power (Marchese 2017). Many of the issues that the singer thematises are taboos, stigmatised and, thus, considered as *uncomfortable*. She has addressed misogyny, homophobia, and racism inside and outside the entertainment industry. In turn, "the fans reflect things back at [her] that make [her] realize they want to talk about the same emotions and issues [she] [wants] to talk about" (Amos in Marchese

2017). Amos reads their "letters" and "[learns] how people see the world," namely through "many different perspectives" (Amos in Marchese 2017). And she recounts that her audiences' powerful (hi)stories have informed her song-writing (Amos 2020, 135). In the more than five decades of her life, however, often regarded as having agency but not the authority to speak up, the artist has been assaulted, ridiculed, and rejected. She has been silenced, by our societies in general, by record companies and the music press in particular.

I could not do justice to Amos' extensive body of artwork within the limited scope of this chapter – if at all. Therefore, as mentioned before, my delineations do not focus on one of her songs or her memoir *Resistance* (2020) in its entirety either. Instead, centring around forms of resistance to gender-based violence on a micro level, my considerations are meant to sketch how Amos' describing forms and patterns of violence in her music and literature can be regarded as a means of personal *and* political defiance. To put it another way, her work can be conceived of as filling "gaps in collective hermeneutical resources" (Fricker 2007, 6). Drawing on elements of Miranda Fricker's conceptual framework of "epistemic injustice", I consider how Amos' sharing her lived experience with violence has established relations among members of imagined communities (2007, 1). These seem to feel understood as well as represented by Amos – and in their shared (hi)stories. Albeit potentially painful, the artist choses to become vulnerable through her pieces of music and writing. And her breaking her silence has encouraged others to share their own embodied (hi)stories of violence.

Miranda Fricker understands *collective hermeneutical resources* as a body of shared meanings that societies produce, not only to understand their own experiences, but also to express and share their understandings with other human beings (2007, 147–148). What she describes as "gaps" in our "hermeneutical resources", i.e. "in our shared tools of social interpretation", re-/create "cognitive [disadvantages]", and it is "no accident that these disadvantages "[impinge] unequally on different social groups" (2007, 6, 151). In an echo of Foucault's theories on order, discourses, and practices, we can assume that, due to one-sided narratives and trans-generational hierarchies, a society's shared meanings –

in other words, our (hi)stories – are mainly produced by and predominately benefit its powerful members (Foucault 1980, 93; Foucault 1995, 140, 170–171, 191, 217). In patriarchy, capitalism, and (post-)colonialism, these are mostly the human *norms* and, thereby, e.g., male, heterosexual, and/or white authorities.

Particularly religious, medical, and colonial discourses have created stories centred around metaphorical concepts, namely narratives that depict, e.g., female, colonised, and homosexual characters conceptualised as the sinful, irrational, dangerous, and/or less-than-human *others*. If they are re-/presented at all. In the same vein as these institutional discourses, stories told through music become part of and trans-/form our affective makeup and accumulated knowledge. As we get to know, establish an emotional connection with, and embody pieces of music, melodies and lyrics can become part of our selves and our (hi)stories. However, for one thing, when, whose, and what kind of stories are told – or remain untold – depends on social, cultural, and historical frameworks, on the privileged perspective of the authors and (self-proclaimed) authorities. In general, these conditions seem to be re-/produced by *embodied audio-visual hierarchies*. For another thing, if authors and their stories are considered as valuable, reliable, and credible is dependent on our belief, value, and evaluative systems. In western societies, patterns of violence and the "economy of credibility" (Fricker 2007, 1) still affect *the others*, for instance those perceived as female, non-western, transgender, and/or past the age of childbearing, much more adversely than the authorities that are mostly constituted by *the norms*, e.g. male, cisgender, and siring colonisers.

In my mind, we experience embodied audio-visual hierarchies, e.g., within public hierarchical structures as they re-/generate and are manifested in the number and percentage, the spacial position, the scope, but also the perceived status of human beings. They illustrate our social orders. As they show us, quite plainly, who has the authority to speak, the right to be heard and listened to, they convey who is allowed to become and remain audible and visible. I conceptualise these self-replicating and multimodal organisational structures as a product and a manifestation of the interrelations among implicit perceptions. At the same time, they appeal to multiple senses in turn. Basically, embodied audio-visual hierarchies are part and parcel of authorship and visibility. They co-/produce our epistemological and ontological frameworks; they co-/create our belief, value, and evaluative systems. They also rely on the effect of the disciplining, medical, and/or colonial gaze (Foucault 2003, 29, 48, 54; Foucault 1995,143, 154, 170). We perceive these impressive power dynamics at home, at the hospital, school, and university, in a conference room, in parliament and church, in the food service industry and the health care sector. We seem to internalise them through and via an ever-growing multi-layered fabric of diverse *percepts*, e.g. through and via our sensations, emotions that we recognise in others, objects and phenomena that we perceive, but also (metaphorical) concepts in our minds, i.e. concepts that rely on and revive (culture-specific) values and interpretations (Niehus-Kettler 2022).[2] Hence, we experience and embody our power structures in the blink of an eye, in the course of our lifetime, and over generations. Inevitably, embodied audio-visual hierarchies manifest in the identities of our authorities and condition the identities of the authors of and protagonists in medical, political, and legal discourses. They also effect and are affected by lacks of diverse perspectives, lacks of self-definitions and self-/representations in media reports, the literary canon, in films – and in popular music. Above all

---

2   The different meanings and conceptualisations of 'percept' are highly dependent on which discipline defines the term, e.g. philosophy, psychology, or linguistics (Lyons 2017). To allow for intra-personal and interpersonal discrepancies among our percepts I need to include all of the understandings and definitions of 'percept' and use it as an umbrella term: a "recognisable sensation or impression received by the mind through the senses" (Harper Collins dictionary online, American English, definition 1); a recognition of emotions (Li 2015, 92); an "object or phenomenon that is perceived" (Harper Collins dictionary online, British English, definition 2); and a 'concept' in our minds (Harper Collins Dictionary online, British English, definition 1). *Metaphorical* concepts appear to be a powerful combination of percepts that also re-/generate our concepts of *the others*. While they are grounded in and, in turn, affect our tacit knowledge and experiences, they also structure our conscious thought and actions (Lakoff and Johnson 2003, 3).

else, such hierarchies re-/generate silences and invisibility. They seem to be the sources and symptoms of fictional stories about *the others'* lacking rationality and credibility. These are (hi)stories fabricated and told, almost exclusively, by the purportedly knowledgeable and righteous *norms* (Niehus-Kettler 2022, 63–63).

Ultimately, I perceive these embodied circumstances as begetting, nurturing, and manifesting in what Fricker explains to be "two forms of epistemic injustice" (2007, 1). Constituting "a wrong done to someone specifically in their capacity as a knower," she "[calls] them testimonial injustice and hermeneutical injustice" (2007, 1).

> Testimonial injustice occurs when prejudice causes a hearer to give a deflated level of credibility to a speaker's word; hermeneutical injustice occurs at a prior stage, when a gap [in collective interpretive resources] puts someone at an unfair disadvantage when it comes to making sense of their social experiences (Fricker 2007, 1).

Fricker (2007) describes, for example, the experiences of two women who lived through *postpartum depression* and *sexual harassment* respectively. These experiences might be conceived of as representing and as being caused by different forms of violence affecting these women's bodies. Still, they can be understood as forms of violence that, in very similar ways, involve epistemic, physical, and psychological violence and harm. Fricker writes that the woman who "[suffered] sexual harassment prior to the time when we had this critical concept" could not "properly comprehend her own experience, let alone render it communicatively intelligible to others" – namely for the very reason that she was not familiar with the concept or comparable (hi)stories of violence (2007, 6). It was "strongly in [both women's] interest to understand" their experiences; however, for lacks of shared stories and, thus, interpretive resources "[they] were left deeply troubled, confused, and isolated" (Fricker 2007, 151). Consequently, they were also "vulnerable" to self-blame and "continued harassment" (Fricker 2007, 151). In a like manner, our "economies of credibility" negatively impacted on their reputation and bodily autonomy (Fricker 2007, 119–120, 147, 149, 151).

Controlling our narratives – and, thereby, controlling what and whose stories are told *or* remain untold – seems more vital to the legitimacy of our bodily autonomy and the legitimacy of our power structures than ever. And popular culture re-/creates and disseminates powerful stories indeed. Conversely, popular media "allow an insight into both the political processes that normalise (certain forms of) violence and the processes that permit the re-cognition of violence *as violence* in everyday life" (Sheperd 2013, 6, author's emphasis). In Amos' self-/representations, the "concepts" "gender and violence" "are in part rendered intelligible through their positioning in relation to other concepts, particularly metaphysical concerns about order and being and questions about moral philosophy regarding legitimacy, justice and truth" (Sheperd 2013, 6). As mentioned before, "[s]ome [of her] stories are highly specific to their social and political context, and some stories have wider resonance" (Sheperd 2013, 3). In *Gender, Violence and Popular Culture: Telling Stories*, Laura J. Sheperd suggests that "our cognitive frameworks are (re)produced in and through the stories we tell ourselves and others" (2013, 3). Drawing on Roland Barthes, she asserts that our "numberless" "narratives, [...] whether we call them myths, tales, fables, history, journalism or discursive formations [...] are all stories. *We are all stories*" (2013, 3, author's emphasis). As Amos places the lyrical bodies of her songs in the matrix of her life stories, her memoir *Resistance* could be read as a metararrative, her "Song Beings" as embedded stories (2020, 37). All of which may be conceptualised as narratives embodied by and within her *and* her audiences. As a form of resistance, these stories are shared and become a part of her and other people's conceptual frameworks and identities. What is more, they can be conceived of as becoming a part of our "collective hermeneutical resources" (Fricker 2007, 147–148). In the end, Amos' writing might be a way to break cycles of abuse on both an intra-personal and an interpersonal level.

Breaking Silences and Breaking Cycles

Reminiscent of Kate Bush's giving the character 'Kathy' from Bronte's *Wuthering Heights* a voice in and through her song of the same title (Mathews 2019), Tori Amos has re-interpreted songs mothered by male artists and given them a female voice on her album *Strange Little Girls*. She is aware of the power of authorship; she knows how different interpretations of (musical) narratives and (hi)stories can affect our sense of self. Also, not unlike many political songs in the 1960s and 1970s, Amos' works are just as much a valuable response to as they are provocations for conversations. This could be conversations about trauma, bodily autonomy, precarity, about who takes part in and becomes part of art and aesthetics. Above all else, with her music and memoirs, Amos portrays affective, but thereby also abusive relationships defined by various forms of violence on a micro, meso, and macro level.

As mentioned before, when Amos refers to pieces of music, she often anthropomorphises. She writes, "Songs are living, breathing things," she describes them as speaking to her, as guiding her (2020, 37, 38). She talks of their "bones" (2020, 124), explains how they possess "power" (2020, 117). For example, circling back to the beginning of this chapter, i.e. to "Girl", we can conceive of the song as embodying a story about the abuse of power. "Girl" might be regarded as telling us about power imbalances and patterns of violence – but also about empowerment. Amos explains that "she" "had not yet been written", but that "Girl" "was with [her] forming herself into a Song Being" while the singer was "battling powerful forces against potential song demolitions" (her first solo album had just been rejected by her label Atlantic Records) (Amos 2020, 37, 38). In fact, the artist feels that songs "present themselves differently" and that they "step forward" at different times in her life (2020, 125).

The song that appears around half-way through the book *Resistance* is "Silent All These Years" (1992) (2020, 17). Amos' readers may meet this song at the heart of her memoir that was published in 2020 because she still feels "Silent" to be "one of the most important songs to [her] personally" (2020, 37, 38, 117). "Without her, I would not be writing to you now. She was the life support that helped me survive a severe personal and artistic crisis" (Amos 2020, 117). The artist recounts that "Silent All These Years" "showed [her] that there were forces [deliberately trying] to silence people" (2020, 117).

> And in that nefarious act of silencing us, we may lose our courage to speak up. And in doing so we would accomplish their censoring for them. If you or I mute ourselves, we have been threatened or shamed into silence. And once again the perpetrators, bullies, and predators steal and possess the narrative, claiming they are the real victims [...]. The art of silencing someone is a dark art indeed (Amos 2020, 117).

Amos adds that "[t]he thought of a person being silenced is scarily as relevant [...] in 2020 [...] as it was when the song [...] was written thirty years ago" (2020, 117).

Tellingly, we find "Silent All these Years" back-to-back with the lyrical body of "Me and a Gun", a song that encompasses what seems to be the circular thoughts of a person being raped. However difficult it must have been, Amos broke her silence one day. The song is about her "own experience as a survivor" of sexual violence (Rozek 2020). Looking back, the singer remembers creating the album "Little Earthquakes", which features "Silent All these Years" and "Me and a Gun", as an "arduous climb to song-write [her] way out of a very personal hell" (Amos 2020, 118). While "writing songs [that were] personal to [her,] the issue of sexual assault [was] blowing up in the political world. The personal [was] political" (Amos 2020, 117, 118). Whereas "Silent" was not meant to be a "political call to action, it became one" as women all around her were facing a "highly charged gender divide" during the autumn of 1991 (Amos 2020, 118). Amos witnessed the humiliation that so-called victims of gender discrimination and sexual violence, such as Anita Hill, were experiencing. At this time, "Hill gave voice to being a survivor of sexual harassment. A woman of colour, she faced a panel of fourteen white men on the Senate Judiciary Committee and said, 'I could not keep silent'" (2020, 118). "'Silent All these Years' would speak to this" – as would "Me and a Gun" (Amos 2020, 118).

The memoir, as an embodied and unfolding metanarrative, the "Song Beings", the (hi)stories, and concepts give meaning to one another – be it through their ways of being re-/presented by Amos, or their having presented themselves at different times in her life (Amos 2020, 125). Moving forward through the author's multi-layered thought structures, we see the lyrics of "Silent All these Years" and "Me and a Gun" connected to a powerful anecdote or, in other words, a nexus. It conveys how our allowing ourselves to be vulnerable can establish *meaning*ful and affective relationships among human beings. One day, Amos' works encouraged a member of her audience, a female judge, to share her own (hi)story of violence with the artist. In the audiobook of her memoir, the singer tells us that she hears more and more stories that are very similar to the judge's account of "living a life of torment and cover-up" (2020, 125, 126).[3] And what follows are the descriptions of patterns of (domestic) violence.

In 2009, when the judge talked to Amos backstage, nearly twenty years had passed since the release of the album *Little Earthquakes* (Amos 2020, 125). At the beginning of the private chat, the woman spoke about" a song that she had developed a relationship with, that had been with her on her journey" (Amos 2020, 125). In the course of the conversation, she depicted a couple whose life some people, "looking in from the outside", "viewed with envy" (Amos 2020, 124). While she considered herself as having "'responsible power' in her courtroom," "she felt powerless […] as a victim of domestic violence" (Amos 2020, 126). The survivor wanted Amos "to comprehend her level of shame" (Amos 2020, 126). Still, she "did not tell [Amos] when the abuse started or how long she kept up the lie"; "at a certain point she [had] begun to believe she was worthless, as [her husband] kept beating that thought into her" (Amos 2020, 126). Moreover, she was convinced that "she could not tell any of the people in her social circle as she was positive they would not risk getting involved"

---

3   Based on interviews, we know that it was not the first time a woman took the singer-songwriter into her confidence after a concert (Amos 2020, 134). One of these meetings changed Amos' life and career for good; after a survivor of sexual abuse asked her for help, she became the "first national spokesperson" of RAINN, i.e. the "Rape, Abuse & Incest National Network" (Rozek 2020)

(Amos 2020, 126). So she was silenced, silenced herself, and "began making friends with songs – one of them being [Amos']" (Amos 2020, 127). In
the end, "songs became her confidants" (Amos 2020, 127).

The judge felt that a song Amos co-created "had given her something
and she wanted to give back" (Amos 2020, 126). The artist thanked her
and replied, "We may be talking about a specific song that was with you
through this nightmare, but while you are speaking, seeds are being
planted for future songs" (2020, 127). And, in fact, the first one of these
songs came into being as "Shattering Sea", which features on an album
published two years later (Amos 2020, 135). This way, another survivor's
story, or rather, one piece of her lived experience manifested in a song
cycle by Amos, who feels that the "judge's story helped to inform the
protagonist" in the album *Night of Hunters* (2011) (2020, 135). "At the heart
of the narrative," i.e. the album, "is a woman in crisis" (Amos 2020,
135). The singer explains that the "song cycle pieces together how the
woman lost her self-worth. It was built in the bones of the story that a
woman who saw herself as independent found herself trapped in a 'grid
of disempowerment'" (2020, 135). She narrates,

> The story was influenced by women as well as men who have sur-
> vived abusive relationships and were willing to share with me the
> complex emotions evoked by verbal abuse and violent threats or
> both physical and verbal abuse they had experienced. People spoke
> with me about becoming a shell of their former selves. It became
> clear that with little or no self-confidence left, they felt they had
> very little ability to fight the oppressive controller in their life (Amos
> 2020, 135).

While we see fragments of Amos' songs mirrored in the judge's personal
(hi)story, e.g. "Girl", "Silent All these Years", and "Me and a Gun", we discern fragments of the judge's (hi)story in "Shattering Sea" (Amos 2020,
34, 119, 122, 128). We can also recognise distinct parts of patterns of violence: The need to keep up appearances, the cruelty and isolation, the de-
ceit, the lost sense of self – the bodily experience/s of shame and fear silencing and confining the survivor. Yet, her breaking her silence by talking to Amos can be conceived of as an expression of – and a move to-

wards other forms of – resistance. Within cyclic systems, both Amos' and her fan's (hi)stories begot, nurtured, and manifested in interrelated song (hi)stories, in shared meanings embodied by the survivors in particular, and the singer's audiences in general. On more than one level, they have become small, but very powerful pieces of our *collective hermeneutical resources* (Fricker 2007, 147–148).

In sum, as part of popular culture, Tori Amos and her shared lived experience affect human beings. They re-/generate meaning/s and understanding in ways that so-called *high-brow* culture and academic discourses might simply not. Her stories foster relatability in societies in which individual, structural, and historical violence are hidden and often go unpunished. She co-/establishes relationships among potential allies in patriarchal, capitalistic, and (post)colonial systems that are, by design, weighted in favour of the (self-proclaimed) authorities and, thus, in favour of keeping pre/convictions in place. Until today, most of our widely-circulated narratives are still written and told – and controlled – by those who have the power to abuse their positions of trust. Above all, the composer shares her experiences with gender-based violence from the perspective of a female, ageing, but privileged singer-songwriter. She tells us (musical) stories that predominantly feature female protagonists, very often even versions of her (former) self. Still, she acknowledges that human beings of any gender and, by implication, people with all kinds of perceived identities experience (trans-generational) patterns of violence (Amos 2020, 135). Due to complementary supremacist ideologies, individuals and groups perceived as *the others* are generally more susceptible to forms of violence, though (Fricker 2007, 119–120, 151).

Amos describes the process of her creating pieces of music as, at times, an "arduous climb to song-write [her] way out" (2020, 118). Like many artists before her, she conceptualises writing as a form of resistance and defiance, as moving forward, as a way of surviving forms of violence. It is not only, but most certainly her storytelling that we can conceive of as a way to become and remain vulnerable, heard, and visible. It is a way of breaking her silence and breaking cycles of abuse – for herself and for others. Albeit painful, in the end, our sharing embodied (hi)stories of violence constitutes and contributes to ways of making sense of our experiences. And it might open up new ways of owning ourselves and becoming the self that – sometime, somewhere, somehow – we feel *we* want to be.

References

Amos, Tori. "Shattering Sea." *Night of Hunters*, Deutsche Grammophon, 2011.

Amos, Tori. "Silent All These Years." *Little Earthquakes*, Atlantic Records, 1992.

Amos, Tori. *Resistance: A Songwriter's Story of Hope, Change, and Courage.* New York: Atria Books, 2020.

Amos. Tori. "Girl." *Little Earthquakes*, Atlantic Records, 1992.

Amos. Tori. *Little Earthquakes*, Atlantic Records, 1992.

Amos. Tori. *Night of Hunters*, Deutsche Grammophon, 2011.

Foucault, Michel. *Discipline & Punish: The Birth of the Prison.* New York: Random House Inc., 1995 [1977].

Foucault, Michel. *Power/Knowledge: Selected Interviews and Other Writings 1972–1977.* Brighton, UK: Harvester Press, 1980.

Foucault, Michel. *The Birth of the Clinic.* Translated by A.M. Sheridan. Abingdon: Routledge, 2003 [1973].

Fricker, Miranda. *Epistemic Injustice: Power and the Ethics of Knowing.* Oxford: Oxford UP, 2007.

Harper Collins Dictionary. "percept." *Harper Collins Dictionary.* https://www.collinsdictionary.com/dictionary/english/ percept (20 May 2021).

Jennings, Ros, and Abigail Gardner. "Introduction. Women, Ageing and Popular Music." *'Rock On': Women, Ageing and Popular Music.* Eds. Ros Jennings and Abigail Gardner. Abingdon: Routledge, 2012. 1–15.

Lakoff, George, and Marc Johnson. *Metaphors We Live By.* Chicago: UP of Chicago, 2003 [1980].

Li, Aijun. *Encoding and Decoding of Emotional Speech: A Cross-Cultural and Multimodal Study between Chinese and Japanese.* New York: Springer, 2015.

Lyons, Jack. "Epistemological Problems of Perception." *The Stanford Encyclopedia of Philosophy*. Ed. Edward N. Zalta (2017). https://plato.stanford.edu/archives/spr2017/entries/perception-episprob/>

Marchese, David. "In Conversation/ Tori Amos: The singer-songwriter on how the music industry silences women, what men need to learn about harassment, and a career spent fighting." *Vulture.com*, 2017. https://www.vulture.com/2017/11/tori-amos-native-invader.html

Mathews, Brendan. "On Kate Bush's Radical Interpretation of *Wuthering Heights*." *Literary Hub*, 13 February 2019. https://lithub.com/on-kate-bushs-radical-interpretation-of-wuthering-heights/

Niehus-Kettler, Melinda. "Becoming one of the *Others*: Embodying and eliminating fabricated natures." *Ageing Masculinities, Alzheimer's and Dementia Narratives*. Eds. Heike Hartung, Rüdiger Kunow and Matthew Sweney. London: Bloomsbury Academic, 2022. 53–70. https://doi.org/10.5040/9781350230637.ch-003.

Norfolk City Council. "Power and Control Wheel." *What is domestic abuse?* https://www.norfolk.gov.uk/safety/domestic-abuse/what-is-domestic-abuse/power-and-control-wheel

Nussbaum, Martha C. *Hiding from Humanity: Shame, Disgust, and the Law*. Princeton, New Jersey: Princeton UP. 2004.

Rozek, Christy. "Music Legend Tori Amos on the Moment that Changed Her Life and Career." *RAINN*, 3 December 2020. https://www.rainn.org/news/music-legend-tori-amos-moment-changed-her-life-and-career

Sheperd, Laura J. *Gender, Violence and Popular Culture: Telling Stories*. Abingdon: Routledge, 2013.

Watson, Paul, and Diane Railton. "Rebel without a Pause: The Continuity of Controversy in Madonna's Contemporary Music Videos." *Rock On': Women, Ageing and Popular Music*. Eds. Ros Jennings and Abigail Gardner. Abingdon: Routledge, 2012. 139–154.

Intersectional Ageing
An Anocritical Reading

Nicole Haring

Abstract: *The intersections of gender and age require a critical cross-disciplinary investigation to reveal the complex and ambivalent nature of cultural narratives of gendered ageing as well as making further identity markers, such as race, class, sexual orientation, and disabilities, visible. This chapter proposes Maierhofer's (1995, 2000, 2003, 2004a, 2004b, 2007, 2012, 2019) intersectional and interdisciplinary analytical approach of Anocriticism for a reading of gender and age/ing as constructs in popular culture. It is the aim of this chapter to investigate and deconstruct cultural narratives of gender and age to reveal their socially constructed nature and highlight their potential for subversion and resistance. This anocritical approach, as an understanding of age as a chronological reality as well as a social construct, similar to the understanding of sex and gender, will be applied as an analytical lens in a reading of the contemporary novel Girl, Woman, Other (2019) by Bernadine Evaristo.*

Keywords: *Anocriticism; gender; ageing; generations; intersectionality; gendered ageing; feminist theory; popular culture; Bernadine Evaristo; Girl; Woman; Other*

Introduction

Popular culture, such as television, cinema, music, literature, and social media, shape our everyday lives and our understandings of the social constructs of gender and age. The cultural interconnectedness of gender and age has been evident since the 1990s. However, recognition of age as a cultural category would not have been possible without the introduction of gender as a category of analysis in literary and cultural studies in the decades before. Feminist theory determined the theoretical and methodological basis that led to the establishment of Age/Ageing Studies as a field (Maierhofer 2019). Susan Sontag, the first to address the intersection of gender and age at a conference of the Institute of Gerontology in 1973, identified the "Double Standard of Aging" as applied to men and women. In a feminist tradition, Sontag early on acknowledged "ageing as a social judgement of women rather than a biological eventuality" (Maierhofer 2019, 2). Since the beginning of the 1990s, Anocriticism (Maierhofer) has been the term used for applying Susan Sontag's approach of linking theories of gender and age to cultural and literary analysis to highlight the specificity of ageing as a cultural category.

This chapter discusses the intersections of gender and age by employing Maierhofer's (1995, 2000, 2003, 2004a, 2004b, 2007, 2012, 2019) feminist approach of Anocriticism in an analysis of the contemporary novel *Girl, Woman, Other (2019)* by Bernadine Evaristo, which depicts several Black British female and non-binary protagonists over their lifecourses. An anocritical reading of the novel follows the parameters of highlighting intersectionality within cultural representations to explore narratives that are diverse and which provide insights into realities of gendered ageing often neglected in popular discourse. As the approach was developed in the late 1990s, its applications have been concerned with literary texts from that period and prior. It is the aim of this chapter to demonstrate the relevance an anocritical reading in the context of contemporary popular culture by investigating Evaristo's Booker Prize Winning novel through the four dimensions of Anocriticism developed by Ratzenböck (2020): (1) age and ageing's collective cultural construction and connection to gender, (2) the individual dimension of ageing, (3) peoples' interpretive power and narrative performance concerning age/ing, and (4) age and ageing's potential for resistance and social change (Ratzenböck 2020, 27).

Anocriticism – Intersections of Gender and Age

When Susan Sontag addressed the intersections of ageing and gender in 1972 in her article "The Double Standard of Ageing" and in 1973 at a conference of the Institute of Gerontology, she was the first one to highlight the cultural and social differences of ageing for men and women. In her remarks, Sontag distinguishes between age and ageing and hence describes old age as "a genuine ordeal, one that men and women undergo in a similar way" and growing older as "an ordeal of the imagination – a moral disease, a pathology – intrinsic to which is the fact that it afflicts women much more than men" (Sontag 1972, 31–32). Thus, Sontag has early on addressed the social and cultural narratives that haunt women and men differently when growing old. Addressing these social perceptions, an understanding was evoked that highlighted the particular intersection of gender and age in social and cultural representations.

Following Sontag's pivotal work, Anocriticism has been the term used since the 1990s in cultural gerontology to discuss the intersections of gender and age (Maierhofer 1995). Maierhofer has explored US-American cultural representations, including novels, short stories, films, and biographies to create a feminist framework that allows for a systemic analysis of gendered ageing that highlights the individual potential for resistance and subversion of heteronormative and limiting assumptions of ageing (Maierhofer 2004a, 320). The exploration of the negotiation of identities is a significant component of an anocritical analysis. American literature was thus the ideal terrain to develop such an approach, as it is, firstly, characterized by diverse texts, which provide intersectional depictions of old women that create diverse narratives; and, secondly, US-American culture is highly individualized, where transgressions of social norms are encouraged (Maierhofer 2003, 33, 2007, 121). Maierhofer (2004a) has further argued that particularly American literature depicts identity as being discussed in "terms of possibilities as well as limitations of the individual within social boundaries, leading to the necessity of narrating the search of the self within the social context as an expression of this identity" (320).

Moreover, the approach aims at "linking theories of gender and age in search of a specific culture of aging" (Maierhofer 2019, 3). Elaine Showalter's term *gynocriticism* (1977, 1985) – a study of women writers and their history, styles, themes, genres, and structures – and Germaine Greer's term *anophobia* (1992) to define the fear of old women influenced the development of Anocriticism as a "method to trace the aspect of aging in cultural representations, the stories we tell ourselves, in order to generate understanding of what it means, in Margaret Morganroth Gullette's (2004) term, to be 'aged by culture'" (Maierhofer 2019, 3). Furthermore, Anocriticism demands a distinction between chronological age and cultural stereotypes associated with old people, following feminist theories' distinction between sex (biological) and gender (cultural). As an inherently feminist approach, Anocriticism thus insists on a deconstruction of binaries to escape the confining oppositions of young and old, and of male and female. Similar to race, class, and gender, age is not understood as flowing naturally or inevitably from the individual biological body but having cultural and social meanings at a particular place and time. What is considered 'young' in a certain place at a certain time depends largely on the difference to what is considered 'old.' Moreover, the relationality between the two notions is apparent and leads to the conclusion that what is considered 'age neutral/universal' in a patriarchal-capitalist society is often implicitly young and male and exclusive of the old, female and other gender identities (Maierhofer 2003, 26–27, 2004a, 322, 2004b, 156, 2012, 96, 2019, 3).

In recent years, the approach of Anocriticism travelled across disciplines and Ratzenböck (2020) developed it further by determining four crucial dimensions of it in her sociological analysis of gendered narratives of ICT use in later life: (1) age and ageing's collective cultural construction and connection to gender, (2) the individual dimension of ageing, (3) peoples' interpretive power and narrative performance concerning age/ing, and (4) age and ageing's potential for resistance and social change (27). An anocritical analysis of any form of text considers all of these four dimensions in the process of interpretation. As Ratzenböck (2020) argues regarding Anocriticism's first analytical dimension, two points are particularly relevant. Firstly, as age and ageing are culturally constructed, they actually transmit little information about an individual per se (Maierhofer 2003, 42, 2007, 113, 2012, 100). Secondly, if we consider age and ageing to be culturally constructed, this implies that they are neither inherently 'good,' nor 'bad,' but that their interpretation depends on collectively shared meanings in specific cultural and social contexts. Thus, it is paramount that any investigation of ageing considers the basic difference between chronological and cultural age. This perspective allows for a nuanced exploration of how common understandings of age are actively produced and reproduced by writers and readers of literature alike, as well as other social agents in society (Maierhofer 2003, 27; Ratzenböck 2020, 27).

However, importantly, Anocriticism also highlights age and ageing's individual dimension (Maierhofer 2003, 53–54). The lives and experiences of older women are diverse and multi-faceted. As Maierhofer (2003) states, in fact, there simply is no single reality accessible to *all* old women (342). For this reason, any analysis of representations of age and/or ageing also needs to explore and trace individual experiences of ageing. Therefore, an anocritical analysis acknowledges the "authority of the individual female experience of age and aging" (Maierhofer 2003, 26, 2007, 115; Ratzenböck 2020, 28). In doing so, Anocriticism foregrounds people's interpretative power and narrative performance in relation to age and ageing by recognizing also their agency and creative sense-making competencies over the life-course (Maierhofer 2003, 53). At all stages of life, individuals continuously need to narrate, interpret, and re-interpret their biographies to maintain a coherent sense of self (Maierhofer 2007, 118). Anocriticism encourages in-depth exploration of these narrative efforts (Ratzenböck 2020, 28).

Finally, Anocriticism implies a focus on age and ageing's potential for resistance and change. As ageing, similar to gender, is culturally constructed, it can also be de-constructed (Maierhofer 2012, 100–101). As a feminist approach, Anocriticism promotes self-determination and transgression of age concepts in analysis of cultural representations as well as in society more broadly. Particularly literary texts may offer a subversive potential in terms of creating and portraying 'counter world[s]'. Analysing these imaginaries highlights that our realities can be changed (Maierhofer 2007, 114–126). Any anocritical analysis thus needs to follow Fetterley's (1977) understanding of being a "resisting reader", which implies focusing on "transgressing rather than the codification of meaning" (Maierhofer 2004b, 157, Ratzenböck, 2020, 29–30).

Therefore, the approach encourages a critical narrative analysis that challenges the status-quo that is based on masculine heteronormative and often times stereotypical notions of gender and age by investigating the complexities and ambivalences present in narratives. Hence, an anocritical reading opens up the possibility to view female ageing as an individual quest filled with contradictions and resistance. The possibilities to develop a sensual relationship with the individual ageing body occurs within the readings of ageing female narratives that question social norms by allowing their individuality to flourish while ageing in a society that regards male youth as the default and makes older women invisible. Addressing the individual narratives through a critical investigation of their time and place, Anocriticism provides the necessary tools for feminist resistance by pinpointing the acts of subversion and protest that are possible through ageing (Maierhofer 1999, 130, 2015, 112). Hence, Anocriticism declares the knowledge of one's possibilities as well as limitations as a political act of resistance (Maierhofer 2019, 7).

Moreover, Anocriticism draws on feminist theoretical premises of intersectionality. The term was first coined by Kimberlé Crenshaw in her legal discussion of Black women in 1989 to visualize the metaphorical intersection of identity markers which construct individual identities, but can be traced back as early as the 19th century. In 1851, Sojourner Truth made her now famous claim of "Ain't I a woman" at a women's convention addressing the livelihoods of Black female slaves and their exclusion in the discussion of women's right during the time. During different social movements, the discussion of interlocking and interdependent systems of oppression were apparent and led feminist discussions toward the now well-known approach of intersectionality. Since its entry into feminist scholarship, intersectionality has gained popularity across disciplines. Its epistemological and methodological debates are informed by the different experiences of women, Black people, Latinx, poor people, LGBTQIA+ people, disabled people, and older people (Hill Collins 2019, 157). By doing so, intersectionality "addresses the most central theoretical and normative concern within feminist scholarship: namely, the acknowledgement of differences" (Davis 2011, 45).

However, intersectionality has also displayed its limitations mainly due to the vagueness of its construction and applicability. In this context, Cho, McCall, and Crenshaw (2013) address the "eponymous 'et cetera' problem" of intersectionality, as the concept often problematizes the "number of categories and kinds of subjects (e. g. privileged or subordinate) stipulated or implied by an intersectional approach" (787). Hence, focusing within an analysis on distinct intersecting identity markers whilst displaying an intersectional consciousness has proven to be an ideal strategy to contribute to intersectional scholarship (Hill Collins 2019, Davis 2011, Lykke 2011). Anocriticism can thus be viewed as a meaningful intersectional contribution. It provides a defined framework with its four dimensions (age and ageing's collective cultural construction and connection to gender, the individual dimension of ageing, peoples' interpretive power and narrative performance concerning age/ing, and age and ageing's potential for resistance and social change (Ratzenböck 2020, 27)) to look at the intersections of age and gender while regarding other identity markers as well. Therefore, a valuable route to intersectional thinking is laid out that contributes to what Hearn and Wray (2015) declare as the challenge "to theorize the interconnections of age, gender(s), sexualities, ethnicities, and other social divisions, and their location in time, place and culture" (206). The following Anocritical reading will pinpoint these interconnections to analyse how an assertion of identity is presented through the protagonists' negotiations of their own gendered and racialised ageing narratives.

An Anocritical Reading of *Girl, Woman, Other* (2019)

Girl, Woman, Other contests "the linear narratives of patriarchal and imperial discourse" (Sánchez-Palencia 2021, 3) by telling the stories of eleven Black women and one non-binary Black person from different generations living in today's Great Britain. Moreover, *Girl, Woman, Other* poses contemporary questions on the intersections of race, class, gender, sexual orientation, and age. In a recent interview about her Booker Prize winning novel, Bernadine Evaristo reflects upon the persisting void of Black British literary voices and describes the aim of her work as to "put presence into absence", by which she emphasises her objectives to change the literary landscape with her diverse protagonists and displays of Black British womanhood (Evaristo in Sethi 2019). To highlight Britain's diversity, the author employs the narrative technique of *multiperspectivity* (also called 'polyperspectivity') to present a mere presence of several stories and viewpoints (Hartner 2014). A polyphonic text is created where each of the twelve protagonists receives their own section within the first four chapters of the book followed by a chapter called the "After – Party" and an epilogue. By doing so, *Girl, Woman, Other* displays a spatial and temporal expansion over different continents and centuries that transgresses normative assumptions of race, class, gender, sexual orientation, and age.

This transgression is further emphasized by the form of the novel. The author calls the style of the novel "fusion fiction", which can be best described as an avant-garde technique that leaves out full stops at the end of sentences and lets the written word flow over the page. Certain parts of the novel, therefore, appear as if they were small poems through the display of their words (Evaristo in Sethi 2019). The boundless writing style provides the possibilities for the individual narratives of the protagonists to fuse into each other within the designated chapters. By doing so, traditional writings styles, such as the usage of punctuations and cohesive paragraphs, are neglected and a unique form is created that supports the content and intention of the author to present non-conforming and unconventional life-stories. Moreover, the "fluid way" of the book replicates that the protagonists' "roots are all over the place," as Evaristo describes the connection between style and history of her characters in a recent interview (Sethi 2019). Finally, this technique enables the protagonists to develop in all their complexities and ambivalences as their narratives take up space on the pages of the book.

The first chapter is divided into the stories of Amma, her daughter Yazz, and her friend Dominique. It depicts the life-stories of two queer theatre directors and former actors who are now in their fifties narrating their lives on the fringes of the British art scene founding their own theatre companies and experiencing misogyny and racism during their early years. Amma describes her younger self as "a renegade lobbing hand grenades at the establishment that excluded her" (Evaristo 2019, 2). Together with her friend Dominque, they "believed in protest that was public, disruptive and downright annoying to those at the other end of it" (Evaristo 2019, 2). Years of hard work filled with numerous rejections last "until the mainstream began to absorb what was once radical and she found herself hopeful of joining it /which only happened when the first female artistic director assumed the helm of the National" (Evaristo 2019, 2) and one of her plays is accepted at the most prestigious theatre in London. Her play is about fierce female African fighters which will be staged in the final chapter of the novel. Although she finally receives the recognition for her artistic work from the mainstream art scene, "Amma will always be anything but normal and as she's in her fifties, she's not old yet" (Evaristo 2019, 3). Transgressing societal beauty norms, Amma wears her hair in what she describes as "peroxide dreadlocks that are trained to stick up like candles on a birthday cake" (3), which her daughter recently described as "a mad old woman look" (Evaristo 2019, 4). Using an ageist and sexist trope to describe her mother's extravagant hair and dressing style, Yazz emphasises how her mother counters stereotypical assumptions of middle-aged women. Her daughter's remark also does not bother Amma, rather encourages her to continue to resist societal norms on various levels and to celebrate getting older (Evaristo 2019, 4).

Although she was often rendered invisible as a Black gay woman in a society that values white male heterosexuality, Amma shows how growing older enabled her to leave cultural assumptions of heteronormative gender roles behind. She never aimed to confirm to societal roles when it came to relationships and she always "saw commitment to one person as imprisonment" (Evaristo 2019, 20) highlighting the constrains of societal norms by using the metaphor of a prison. Nevertheless, she decided in her thirties to have a child with a close friend, which she calls her "counterculture experiment" (Evaristo 2019, 36). The experience made her commit to conventional norms and realize that it actually completed her, which was hard to confess at first as it seemed "somehow anti-feminist" (Evaristo 2019, 36), but also displays the ambivalences of lives. In addition, Amma describes how her sexual longings also changed over the years, where she finds herself now in her fifties "craving the intimacy that comes from being emotionally, although not exclusively, close to another person" (Evaristo 2019, 21). Her continuous discovery of her sensual self and her own negotiation of her sexuality remain present elements in Amma's life which she has managed to cater to by having two partners who are independent women and even know each other. Overall, Amma's narrative breaks with conventional maternal narratives of the asexual mother who disguises her sensuality, but rather displays a contradicting narrative of a middle-aged woman which flourishes in its ambivalences and discontinuities.

The second section of the novel continues with telling three entangled life-stories of Carole, her Nigerian mother Bummi, and her classmate LaTisha. Particularly Bummi's narrative amplifies the individualized dimension of ageing and one's narrative power to challenge cultural constructs of ageing. Her narrative problematizes the intersections of gender, race, class, sexual orientation, and age. Migrating to Great Britain with a university degree, she imagined better opportunities in the job market, but soon realizes "that her first class degree from a Third World country would mean nothing in her new country especially with her name and nationality attached to it" (Evaristo 2019, 167). When her husband passes away and she is left alone to take care of her daughter, the economic hardship combined with their migratory background leaves a mark on her, but at the same time encourages her to follow her dream of founding her own cleaning company, despite what her close environment thinks of the idea. Lacking the financial resources to do so, she asks the local pastor for financial support, which he only provides in return for sex. Bummi accepts the offer describing it as "her first transaction as a businesswoman" (Evaristo 2019, 173), but later swears to herself that "she would never tell anyone how low she had gone to elevate herself and her daughter" (Evaristo 2019, 174). The contradictions of life are displayed in the incident where the protagonist feels powerful and powerless at the same time in order to overcome her burdens.

Moreover, Bummi's story is filled with unexpected turns and surprises that resist normative assumptions of older women. For her company, she hires her friend Omofe and soon starts a secret love relationship with her. Trapped in her own heterosexual normativity, their relationship is portrayed, on the one hand, as very intimate, when Bummi states that she "felt tingles down the side of her body that blended into Omofe" and that "Omofe felt like home to Bummi and her expert activities culminated in the most intense pleasure" (Evaristo 2019, 179). Yet, on the other hand, Bummi's uneasiness for being with a woman instead of a man interferes with her feelings for Omofe: "the shame she tried to suppress began walking towards her /she did not want to be that sort of person/it was not who she was" (Evaristo 2019, 180). Soon her worries drive her away from her girlfriend. Unable to accept her desire for a woman, Bummi decides to leave Omofe, and eventually finds a new male partner again with whom she eventually spends the rest of her life. Nevertheless, Bummi's story depicts how individual life-stories are often complex and discontinuing. Breaking with her own principles to elevate herself and her daughter socially shows the resistance in Bummi's character, but also how vulnerability accompanies this act of resistance. Moreover, it is visible in her story that "racialized aging bodies from low income backgrounds may entail multiple layers of exile and invisibility" (Rajan-Rankin 2018, 34), but that the individual dimension of ageing makes it possible to challenge collective heteronormative assumptions of ageing Black women.

Following Bummi's story, the third chapter depicts the life-stories of Shirly, her mother Winsome, and her colleague Penelope, where each of them highlights the different experience of growing up as Black women in Great Britain mediating what it means to live in a certain time at a certain place. Different generations have different opportunities, which Shirly and her mother Winsome represent in particular. Winsome migrated with her husband Clovis to Great Britain's country side, where there were no Black people common there. Thus, they were met with great hostility and a lack for work and support from the local community there. Continuously, they were denied residence or service and were met with outright racism and hostility. Although Clovis wanted to remain there due to his love for nature and the country side more generally, the societal constrains and daily abuse targeted at them led the young couple eventually to settle down in London, where the anonymity of the big city life paired with a greater diversity of cultures, races, and ethnicity was more welcoming. In the city, the couple worked endlessly to create a better life for their children in a country where their skin colour continues to be seen as *Other*. Reminiscing about their hardship after their immigration to Great Britain, Winsome has a hard time relating to her daughter's discomfort with her job as a teacher as she sees it as an act of being ungrateful for their efforts to provide a good life for them.

The depiction of the mother-daughter relationship is complicated and finds its peak in the narrative when Winsome shares the intimate details about her affair with Lennox, her daughter's husband. Finding him only attractive at first, he shows up one day at her doorstep "and so it continued for over a year /once a week, sometimes twice" (Evaristo 2019, 273). Their secret makes Winsome question "who was this woman letting her son-in-law do her every which way?" (Evaristo 2019, 272) emphasizing their wild affair and her newly discovered sensuality. She also questions her own perception of herself as an older woman, who finds herself now in a secret and intense sexual relationship with a younger man, who is erotically drawn to her ageing body. After years of being determined by her maternal roles ("first she was a daughter, then a wife and mother, and now also a grandmother and great-grandmother" (257)), Winsome decides that "she deserved to have this/him" (273). The decision may appear as selfish on the surface but reveals deeper layers as the protagonist reflects on the suppression of her own desires over the years of confirming to maternal societal norms and to live up to her family's expectation as the selfish care-taker. Finally, Winsome experiences a sense of selfhood that enables her to make the decision to continue the affair whilst being aware that she finds herself in a moral dilemma that will hurt her daughter's feelings. To calm her doubts, she comes up with an explanation for herself that it is still better she satisfies the needs of her son-in-law rather than some strange woman. Yet, eventually the affair drifts away and they return to being in-laws again. Similar to Bummi, Winsome's narrative shows her ageing as a road to her sensual self and a way of expressing her sexual feelings. Both women have raised children and been married, and yet share in their narratives their most intimate selves to highlight how intersections of age, gender, race, and sexuality are mediated to problematize heteronormative assumptions of what it means to grow old as a woman. By doing so, they destabilize gender norms, show their vulnerability in their resistance and make thus room for new gendered life narratives (Butler 2016, 18).

Finally, the fourth and last chapter of the novel tells the stories of a resilient Black genealogy of Megan, who later becomes Morgan, Hattie, and Grace. Hattie, who is the oldest character in the book with 93-years of age, provides another individualised dimension of what it means to grow old for women. As a Black farmer in the countryside in England, her life was marked by exclusion and inclusion. She presented an *Otherness* that allowed her to thrive on her own terms, but at the same time was met with reluctance and hostility by the society of the time who was very wary of the first Black woman farmer on the British countryside running one of the largest farms there. Additionally, Hattie experiences great hardship in her role as mother. Getting pregnant at a very young age from a white boy from the village, her father urges her to give the child up for adoption because he believes that "her life will be forever ruined with a bastard child/ men will have two reasons not to marry you" (370). Her father is a white aristocratic patriarch from rural Great Britain who decides the faith of her new born child and also highlights the racial biases present towards her daughter, although he was madly in love and married to her mother. Eventually, her father passes away and she marries an African-American, who happened to travel through the countryside and fell in love. Together they take over the farm and work on it until his death. Afterwards, she continues to run the farm by herself, which continues to astonish her community on the country side. She shares an experience with officials who would stop by at the farm and "poked their nose around and couldn't hide their surprise at who they saw in charge" (347) emphasizing that her gendered, racialised, and ageing body was not what they have expected to encounter. Ignoring the hostility, she continues to be met with, Hattie lives her live on her own terms and finds great joy in deciding for herself how to live her life as a widow on a large farm.

The relationship of Hattie and her grandchild Morgan as well as their transgender partner highlights how the different generations are related in their individual quest for identity and belonging. Both characters experience hostility due to their intersecting identities and diverse livelihoods, yet overcoming generational division with regard to political views, their relationship shows how individual narratives of gender and generations can provide possibilities for change. Although Hattie does not fully understand Morgan's gender transformation and her political views, her narrative expresses her own biases and how the protagonists manage to overcome them. First dictated by learned heteronormative perceptions of gender, Hattie eventually embraces Morgan's development and gives her farm to the young couple hoping to transform it into a place for other people to live their truest selves. Overcoming social burdens, Morgan accepts her grandmother's gift with greatest appreciation and finally feels accepted by her kin. By giving Morgan the farm, Hattie realises she will make other family members angry, yet does not dwell on this pressure, but rather sees her final wish as an act of political resistance out of love. Her actions can be read through an anocritical lens to interpret how everyday life decisions present also possibilities to realise social change. Hence, Anocriticism enables the reader to view their interpretative powers to highlight the complexities and ambivalences of gender and generations in cultural narratives at a certain time and place. This possibility can be seen as an act of feminist resistance that contributes to the understanding of what it means to grow old at a certain time and place.

The dominant theme of all four chapters made apparent through an intersectional investigation of the protagonists Amma, Bummi, Winsome, and Hatti is their sexuality and relationship to their racialised and ageing bodies over their life courses. Following feminists' understandings of women's bodies as contested sights of institutional and personal powers, "a discussion of female bodies aware of their own sexuality allows for a repudiation of culturally negative, trivializing stereotypes associated with aging women" (Maierhofer 2004, 322). A new awareness of their bodies is present in the readings of these protagonists' stories, where the first three display it in their sensual relationships with themselves and through sexual relationships to others that often transgress their own perceptions of social conventions. The fourth narrative stresses more her realisation of the constructed nature of gender and sexual identity through her relationship to her grandchild and their partner. This engagement, however, can be seen as an interdependence between the generations that continues the negotiation and growing awareness of what it means to be gendered racialised ageing bodies in a society that renders them invisible. Thus, the investigation aligns with Butler's (2004) claim that "terms of gender designation are thus never settled once and for all but are constantly in the process of being remade" (10), similar to notions of ageing.

Conclusion

Summing up, Maierhofer developed Anocriticism as a distinct feminist approach to investigate the particular intersections of gender and ageing to highlight the intrinsic connection between feminist theory and Age/Ageing Studies. Similar to gender and sex, age is biologically and culturally constructed and provides thus opportunities for deconstruction and re-interpretation of what it means to grow old. As noted by Ratzenböck (2020, 27–29), who outlined four distinct dimensions of the approach, with the help of Anocriticism as a tool to critically analyse narratives, individual dimensions of experiences and representations – in relation to collectively shared meanings – become apparent. People's interpretative power and narrative performance are another crucial dimension of Anocriticism. Both create the potential for resistance and change in everyday life as well as in research. Anocritical explorations of cultural representations of gender and age in popular culture offer 'counter world[s]' (Maierhofer 2007, 118) that allow us all to move beyond established definitions of self. Reading a contemporary novel, such as Bernadine Evaristo's *Girl,*

Woman, Other (2019), through an anocritical lens allows to resist conventional notions of gendered ageing by valuing the individual quest, particular of older women, to their sensual selves and to negotiate their ageing bodies by their own terms resisting societal norms of conventional heterosexual ageing. As the novel highlights intersectionality and relationality, and inhabits an intergenerational character that enables individual narratives to develop and to define on their own complex and ambivalent terms of what it means to age, an Anocritical reading enables an exploration of the complex interplay of individuality and collectivism to demonstrate fictionally "how irreducibly complex social life is" (McCall 2005, 1773).

References

Butler, Judith. "Rethinking Vulnerability and Resistance." *Vulnerability in Resistance*. Ed. Judith Butler, Zeynep Gambetti, and Leticia Sabsay. London: Duke University Press, 2016. 1–27.

Butler, Judith. *Undoing Gender*. New York: Routledge, 2004.

Cho, Sumi, Kimberlé Williams Crenshaw, and Leslie McCall. "Toward a Field of Intersectionality Studies: Theory, Applications, and Praxis." *Signs: Journal of Women in Culture and Society* 38.4 (2013): 785–810.

Crenshaw, Kimberlé. "Demarginalizing the Intersection of Race and Sex: A Black Feminist Critique of Antidiscrimination Doctrine, Feminist Theory and Antiracist Politics." *University of Chicago Legal Forum* 1989.1 (1989):139–167.

Davis, Kathy. "Intersectionality as Buzzword: A Sociology of Science Perspective on what makes a Feminist Theory Successful." *Framing Intersectionality – Debates on a Multi-Faceted Concept in Gender Studies*. Ed. Helma Lutz, Maria Teresa Herrera Vivar, and Linda Supik. London: Routledge, 2011. 43–54.

Evaristo, Bernardine. *Girl, Woman, Other*. London: Penguin Books, 2019.

Fetterley, Judith. *The Resisting Reader: A Feminist Approach to American Fiction*. Bloomington: Indiana University Press, 1981.

Greer, Germaine. *The Change: Women, Ageing and the Menopause*. London: Bloomsbury Publishing, 1992.

Hartner, Marcus. "Multiperspectivity." *The Living Handbook of Narratology*. Ed. Peter Hühn. Hamburg: Hamburg University, 2014. 353–363.

Hearn, Jeff, and Sharon Wray. "Gender: Implications of a Contested Era." *Routledge Handbook of Cultural Gerontology*. Ed. Julia Twigg and Wendy Martin. New York: Routledge, 2015. 201–209.

Hill Collins, Patricia. *Intersectionality as Critical Social Theory*. Durham: Duke University Press, 2019.

Lykke, Nina. "Intersectional Analysis: Black Box or Useful Critical Feminist Thinking Technology." *Framing Intersectionality: Debates on a Multi-Faceted Concept in Gender Studies*. Ed. Helma Lutz, Maria Teresa Herrera Vivar, and Linda Supik. London: Routledge, 2011. 207–221.

Maierhofer, Roberta. "Das Leben Als Narrativer Akt: Altern Als Erzählen'." *Moderne. Kulturwissenschaftliches Jahrbuch 6 (2010/11). Themenschwerpunkt: Alter(n)*. Ed. Helga Mitterbauer and Katharina Scherke. Vienna: Studien Verlag, 2012. 97–111.

Maierhofer, Roberta. "Der Gefährliche Aufbruch Zum Selbst: Frauen, Altern Und Identität in der amerikanischen Kultur. Eine Anokritische Einführung." *Altern in Gesellschaft. Ageing – Diversity – Inclusion*. Ed. Ursula Pasero, Gertrud M. Backes, and Klaus R. Schroeter. Wiesbaden: VS Verlag für Sozialwissenschaften, 2007. 111–127.

Maierhofer, Roberta. "Feminism and Aging in Literature." *Encyclopedia of Gerontology and Population Aging*. Ed. Danan Gu and Matthew E. Dupre. Berlin: Springer, 2019. 1–8.

Maierhofer, Roberta. "Simone de Beauvoir and the Greying of American Feminism." *Journal of Aging and Identity* 5 (2000): 67–77.

Maierhofer, Roberta. "The Greying of American Feminism." *Values in American Society*. Ed. Tibor Frank. Budapest: Eötvös Loránd University, 1995. 113–121.

Maierhofer, Roberta. "The Old Woman as Prototypical American." *What is American? New Identities in U.S. Culture*. Ed. Walter Hölbling and Klaus Rieser. Münster: LIT, 2004a. 319–336.

Maierhofer, Roberta. "Third Pregnancy: Women, Ageing, and Identity in American Culture. An Anocritical Approach'. *Old Age and Ageing in British and American Culture and Literature*, Ed. Christa Jansohn. Münster: LIT, 2004b. 155–171.

Maierhofer, Roberta. *Salty Old Women: Eine anokritische Untersuchung zu Frauen, Altern und Identität in der amerikanischen Literatur*. Essen: Die Blaue Eule, 2003.

McCall, Leslie. "The Complexity of Intersectionality." *Signs: Journal of Women in Culture and Society* 30.3 (2005):1771–1800.

Morganroth Gullette, Margaret. *Aged by Culture*. Chicago: University of Chicago Press, 2005.

Rajan-Rankin, Sweta. "Race, embodiment and later life: Re-animating aging bodies of color." *Journal of Aging Studies* 45 (2018): 32–38.

Ratzenböck, Barbara. *Media Relations – How and Why Older Women Care for Information and Communication Technologies*. 2020. University of Graz, PhD dissertation.

Sánchez-Palencia, Carolina. "Feminist/Queer/Diasporic Temporality in Bernardine Evaristo's *Girl, Woman, Other* (2019)." *European Journal of Women's Studies* (2021):1–15.

Sethi, Anita. "Bernardine Evaristo: 'I Want to Put Presence into Absence.'" *The Guardian, 27 April 2019.* https://www.theguardian.com/books/2019/apr/27/bernardine-evaristo-girl-woman-other-interview#:~:text=What%20were%20your%20motivations%3F.

Showalter, Elaine. *The Female Malady: Women, Madness, and English Culture (1830–1980)*. London: Virago Press, 1985.

Showalter, Elaine. *Towards a Feminist Poetics*. London: Virago Press 1977.

Sontag, Susan. "The Double Standard of Aging." *Saturday Review of the Society* LV. 39 (1972): 29–38.

Truth, Sojourner. "Ain't I a woman?" Akron: Ohio, 1851.

'WhatsApp Aunts'
Ageism, Sexism, and the Marginalisation
of Older People in Brazilian Politics

Mariana Castelli-Rosa and Mariana Lins

Abstract: *The rise of the former far-right Brazilian president Jair Bolsonaro has shed light on his supporters' age aspects thus evidencing his opponents' use of ageist tropes to counter Bolsonaro's discourse. National surveys indicate that many of the government's "die-hard" supporters tend to be men and people over 60. As a result, Bolsonaro's left-wing opponents use ageism coupled with sexism to vilify his electors instead of standing for a more reasonable debate. In our chapter, we analyse how issues of age and gender coincide with the stereotype and meme of "tia do zap" ("WhatsApp aunt") that circulate on the Internet. This stereotype/meme contrues right-wing older people as people who spread fake news on social media. By examining the left's and right's use of this stereotype in Brazil, we problematize them both, highlighting the lack of intersectionality from the left. While the meme is an ageist oversimplification, it also indicates that old people's support for Bolsonaro coincides with their retrieval of political and social agencies. We also present the political background of Brazil; discuss the far-right's use of social media to disseminate fake news, a factor that reinforces the idea that conservative old people share false information on the Internet; analyse some of the memes; present an example of an older person who has used this stereotype to reclaim her political and social agencies and do a critique of the left to which ageism has become a blind spot.*

Keywords: *ageism; WhatsApp; tia do zap; fake news; politics; gender; Jair Bolsonaro; Brazil; far-right; left-wing*

Introduction

In Brazil, the rise of the far right, a growing distrust in the left, and the lack of conversations about ageism, among other factors, have created the perfect conditions for the appearance of an internet meme based on a stereotype about old people who support former President Jair Bolsonaro. 'Tia do zap'[1] (in English, 'WhatsApp aunt') is a derogatory term that refers to old, right-wing people (both women and men) who are considered to be politically active online. It seems to be an ageist, not to mention sexist, construal of the Brazilian left, as it represents most of President Jair Bolsonaro's supporters as older women who spread fake news on social media. There is some truth to this stereotype in the sense that it indicates Brazilians' increasing use of social media and message applications (apps) to access and read the news.[2] However, the use of social media and message apps alone does not explain the emergence of this stereotype, which later started to circulate as a meme, and, as a result, may have possibly inspired older people to become even more politically active online. The emergence of 'WhatsApp aunts' coincides with the rise of the far right after 2013[3] and their effective yet question-

---

1   In Brazilian Portuguese, WhatsApp is often referred to as 'zap' or 'zap zap'.

2   Most Brazilians get informed online instead of watching the news on TV (Lapper 2021, 38), which was the prevalent media before the popularisation of the internet (Damgaard 2019, 24). A study by the Getúlio Vargas Foundation indicates that by 2018 there were more than 220 million smartphones in use in this country and that Brazilians consult the internet more than 30 times a day (Lapper 2021, 40; Moura and Corbellini 2019, 101). Moreover, according to Pesquisa Globo, 140 million Brazilians access social media platforms ("Pandemia e o Consumo De Notícias Nas Redes Sociais" 2020) and, in 2021, the Digital News Report highlights that, together, Facebook (47%) and WhatsApp (43%) are Brazilians' main source of information (Carro 2021). When it comes to people aged 55 or older, WhatsApp is the platform of choice, closely followed by Facebook and YouTube (Soutto 2021).

3   Richard Lapper (2021, 85) describes the events of June 2013: "What started out at the beginning of the month as a protest against higher bus fares had by the end of the month become a broad-based attack not just on political corruption but on the entire political class itself".

able use of the internet in the 2018 presidential campaign that elected Bolsonaro. More importantly, the term 'WhatsApp aunt' is also an ironic reference to Bolsonaro's use of WhatsApp bulk message senders disseminating mainly fake news to boost his online presence.[4]

In this chapter, we will analyse how issues of age and gender coincide with the meme of 'WhatsApp aunt', which will allow us to explore ageism in Brazilian society and politics. By examining the left's and right's use of this stereotype, we want to problematise them both, but we especially want to highlight the left's lack of critical engagement with their own uses of ageism, which has become a blind spot. We also want to acknowledge that not all older people are conservative. In Brazil, many of those who are considered to be old now were involved in politically progressive agendas such as ending the dictatorship in the 1980s. Moreover, we want to highlight that even though the expression 'WhatsApp aunt' may resonate with the 'OK, Boomer' meme,[5] the former comes from a different context and has a different function as the example of someone who identifies as a 'WhatsApp aunt' and uses this expression to feel empowered will show.

To analyse the phenomenon of 'WhatsApp aunts', we are going to present the political background from which this stereotype and meme emerged. After that, we will discuss the far-right's use of social media to

---

4   In her work on "digital populism," Cesarino (2021, 3) describes the "Whatsapp aunt" as a portion of Bolsonaro's electorate that was gradually captured by the digital apparatus and mechanism of mobilisation created to build his hegemony on- and offline.

5   In the second semester of 2019, after Greta Thunberg's arrival in New York and due to the increasing popularity of her "Fridays for Future" movement in North America, newspapers started to write stories about youth going on school strikes. Initially, they are portrayed as a means for young people to voice their opinions and pressure the government. Soon, the discourse changed as signs from these youth become more aggressive towards older people ("Boomers, we will not forgive you"). However, the intergenerational conflict only became official when the New York Times published a story explaining that the popularity of "OK Boomer" was due to the: "[r]ising inequality, unaffordable college tuition, political polarization exacerbated by the internet, and the climate crisis all fuel anti-boomer sentiment" (Lorenz 2019).

disseminate fake news, a factor that reinforces the idea that conservative old people share false information on the internet and explains, along with the political context, the victory of Bolsonaro. Then, we are going to analyse some of the memes to understand which ideas about older people, especially older women, have been circulating and how these are used in the political discourse. Next, we will discuss the legitimacy of older protesters and how political engagement can be an alternative for marginalised ageing people to regain political and social agencies. We will end the text with a critique of the Brazilian left due to their exclusion of age in debates that strive to be intersectional.

Political Background

On October 28, 2018, Bolsonaro won the election with 55.13% of the votes in the second-round poll. Almost 58 million Brazilians democratically elected the man who, despite his public flirting with authoritarianism, became the leader of the largest South American country, putting an end to years of progressive politics that began in 2003 with the election of Luiz Inácio Lula da Silva, leader of the PT (Workers' Party). Bolsonaro's victory happened in the wake of the parliamentary coup that culminated in the impeachment of President Dilma Rousseff in 2016 and the temporary mandate of then Vice-President Michel Temer.

After this parliamentary coup, the public's distrust of the PT and other left parties became exacerbated. Bolsonaro's allies further encouraged this distrust with fabricated corruption scandals involving former President Lula. This active scandal campaign fragmented the left, which prevented leftists from forming a united front against Bolsonaro. The resulting democratic instability also facilitated the re-emergence of far-right movements that had been apparently dormant since the end of the military dictatorship in 1985. These movements have rarely been held accountable for the damages they caused to the country, due, mainly, to Brazil's 1979 *Lei da Anistia* (Amnesty Law), a dubious attempt to foster democracy that benefited both those who had been politically persecuted and their torturers. In the long run, this law made the Brazilian judicial system incapable of settling matters with the armed forces or even judging crimes committed by and in the name of the Brazilian government. The Amnesty Law, created as an attempt to turn the page, eventually became a tool in the effort to dodge a crucial political debate about the scars that the dictatorship left in Brazilian politics, society, and institutions.

Without proper address and after time, the memory of the military dictatorship became diffuse and even questionable to partisans of conspiracy theories with authoritarian tendencies. They soon found the perfect fora on the internet to discuss topics that the constitutional pact of the re-democratisation after the dictatorship had unofficially banned from politics. Gradually, in face of the rising crisis during Rousseff's government and the consequent distrust in the left that it triggered, the initially timid public support that far-right parties and politicians received turned into a tsunami and generated a crisis of narratives: the 1964 military coup was renamed a "revolution" and torturers became "heroes" that were praised in Congress.[6] At the same time, part of the public increasingly urged for the armed forces to intervene, since purging the Congress and the Supreme Court became, according to them, the main possible solutions for the problems faced by the country. The result is what Machado and Miskolci (2019, 956) call "moral entrepreneurs," that is, right-wing dissidents that use anti-institutional discourses to oppose the debate and advancement of matters related to culture and social conventions. The anti-corruption rhetoric is the main revindication of these moral entrepreneurs, who are often haunted by the imminent possibility of a communist revolution coming to conquer the world (and that is due to start in Brazil) and introduce so-called 'gender ideologies', among other 'monstrosities' that would result in the end of many established institutions such as the patriarchal family and private property.

The strategy of creating an enemy that elicits fear and paranoia has been used before. During the Cold War, for instance, the USA and the

---

6   In 2016, during Rousseff's impeachment hearing, Bolsonaro gave a speech in Congress defending her ousting and dedicating his vote to the memory of Colonel Carlos Brilhante Ustra, one of Rousseff's torturers.

USSR both fabricated enemies to justify the governments' actions and help in the maintenance of nationalism (de Albuquerque and Quinan 2019). A well-known example is McCarthyism, which persecuted screenwriters, actors, directors, musicians, and other professionals of the entertainment industry in Hollywood due to their supposed links to the Communist Party in the USA. Recently, the dissemination of fear and hate to scare 'concerned citizens' has become more elaborate and systematic with the use of message apps and social media platforms. With the massive distribution of fake contents through these media, the voices of far-right movements have become amplified, creating democratic instability not only in Brazil but also in other countries such as the USA, Poland, and Hungary, where authoritarian governments currently prosper or have prospered with the support articulated in the digital world.

A large portion of the far-right material that circulates on social media pertains to fabricated realities and misleading interpretations of facts. These are fake news, which are deceitful or have the aim to misinform the public (Recuero, Bonow Soares, Vinhas, Volcan, Zago, Marchioro Stumpf, Viegas, Hüttner, Bonoto, Silva, Passos, Salgueiro, and Sodré 2021, 10). This content is spread with light speed through social media thanks to the help of technical devices (robots) and humans. In 2020, Patrícia Campos Mello (2020), a reporter of the *Folha de São Paulo* (*FSP*), one of the major dailies in Brazil, investigated the use of the fake news industry during the 2018 presidential electoral campaigns. In her book, she exposes how complex fake news dissemination networks sponsored by those interested in the election of Bolsonaro were able to dodge state juridical apparatuses. The investigative story Campos Mello wrote for *FSP* was crucial to legally contest Bolsonaro's campaign and change the rules about WhatsApp bulk sender services.

'Data-Aunt'

In October 2020, during an interview in a Brazilian TV show, Campos Mello answered why she thinks 'WhatsApp aunts' have credibility (Tas 2020). She mentions that while real news tends to be less spectacular, fake ones generate engagement. Similarly, Ernesto Perini-Santos (2021, 351) highlights that fake news tends to be more "attention-grabbing". In a book about the collapse of democracy in Brazil, Perini-Santos (2021, 343–344) examines how "post-truth", a distrust in institutions that mediates knowledge and information, operates in Brazil. The spread of fake news is a consequence of this distrust, especially on the internet where anybody can produce and share content.

Even though Campos Mello acknowledges the role and relevance of 'WhatsApp aunts' in the fake news machinery created by Bolsonaro and his allies, she does not give them enough attention in her book. It is difficult to say when exactly this expression started to circulate, but, since 2014, Brazilian newspapers have published stories about the popularization of WhatsApp family groups (Fischberg 2014). One study highlights that Brazilians' favourite online pastime is to check WhatsApp group messages (Lapper 2021, 40; Moura and Corbellini 2019, 101). In the context of isolated older people, understanding the creation of public online spaces where they can interact and share news and memes with family members is essential for analysing the advent of this meme and stereotype. In 2015, as Brazilian society increasingly became more polarised after Rousseff's election, merely one year away from her impeachment and with many WhatsApp family groups already consolidated, newspapers started to publish stories using the expression 'WhatsApp aunts' (Cardoso 2015).

It is not the first time that the image of an older woman is used in the Brazilian imaginary. In an article about the intersection of widowhood, memory, oral history, and military dictatorships in Latin America, Lídia M. V. Possas (2011) has noticed an increase in the use of the word "viúva" (in English, 'widowess') in Brazilian newspapers since 2003. The author observes that this word is used loosely and in different political contexts, but, in all of them, it has negative connotations. This implies that 'widowesses' have become near-abject non-beings, forgotten by both the militaries and human rights activists who mainly establish their political agendas with the idea of a family in mind (Possas 2011, 89). In Brazil, a well-known expression is "viúva da ditadura" ('widowess of the dictatorship'), which does not merely refer to a woman whose husband died during the dictatorship in Brazil as it may seem at first. More importantly, this expression refers to those (no matter what gender or age) that miss the dictatorship and want it restored. We did not find any scholarly articles on this specific use of language, which emphasises the left's lack of self-awareness. However, a 2018 story, published by the left-leaning Brazilian Intercept less than a week after Bolsonaro was allegedly stabbed, uses this expression in its headline: 'While Brazil can still elect 'widowesses of the dictatorship,' Chile continues to punish its military' (Brum 2018). This story hints not only at Brazil's lack of commitment to reassessing its past and punish those involved in the dictatorship, but also at the limited discussions among Brazilian left-wingers that exclude gender and age while at the same time othering older women and excluding them of political discussions. With this precedent that it was already acceptable to speak about (older) women in such atrocious terms, it is likely that the term 'WhatsApp aunt' is a development that reflects the current political context and the increasing use of social media.

Moreover, even though we are hesitant and careful not to collapse all older people in the politically conservative category, it is true that Bolsonaro's approval rate among people over 60 is still rather substantial.[7] Since the start of the Covid-19 pandemic and with the deaths of more than 600,000 Brazilians, his support has progressively decreased especially due to his mismanagement of the pandemic and the consequent economic crisis. But, in 2021, during the third year of his term, which, doubtlessly, represents a moment of discontentment even among Bolsonaro voters and supporters, some remain supportive. The 'WhatsApp aunt' is believed to be one of them.

In a 2020 YouTube interview to his son and Congressman Eduardo Bolsonaro, the president recognised the engagement of the 'WhatsApp

---

7   According to PoderData, in September 2021, President Bolsonaro's government is better evaluated by two age groups: those between 25 and 44 years old (30% of them consider it good/great) and those over 60 (28% of them consider it good/great). In other age cohorts, such as 16- to 24-year-olds and 45- to 59-year-olds, only 16% of respondents evaluate Bolsonaro's government as good/great (Lopes 2021).

aunts' and he even attributed the Internet activism that helped him win the 2018 election to them.[8] In the video, he seems upset with the opponents' critique that 'WhatsApp aunts' are an 'alternative' source of information. He emphasises the importance of 'WhatsApp aunts' who defend the government daily and opposes the left's urge to silence them and other websites that distribute news favourable to him. According to the perception of the left and right, 'WhatsApp aunts' are part of the 'die-hard' Bolsonaro supporter core, that is, they are the group of voters that will hardly change their mind, are horrified by left-wing protesters, and take Bolsonaro's 2018 slogan seriously: "Brazil above everything, God above all."

'WhatsApp Aunt' Memes

As seen with the expression 'widowesses of the dictatorship', the left's use of ageism and sexism in the political discourse is not new. In 'WhatsApp aunts', the coupling of age and gender creates another stereotype of old women in a different political context, which again expels older people from the political discourse while, at the same time, tries to explain Bolsonaro's supporters backing of antidemocratic agendas. 'Othering' is a process that identifies certain people as those that do not belong or stand at the margins of society. Through othering stereotypes, or, in the words of Patricia Hill Collins (2000), "controlling images" are created. Hill Collins writes about the stereotypes concerning Black women, whose main function is to justify racial oppression thus perpetuating it (2000, 73), but her insight is helpful to understand how the left's othering operates: By using these stereotypes to marginalise 'older women', their discourse is dismissed with the justification that these are not coherent people.

---

8   The video was removed by YouTube for violating Covid-19 incorrect medical information policies, but the Brazilian daily *Gazeta do Povo* published a story on this interview ("Bolsonaro Celebra 'Tia Do Zap' e Deseja 'Bom Fim De Ano e Excelente 22 Para Todos Nós.'" 2020).

Another important idea about the use of stereotypes comes from Viktor Chagas (2018, 7), who highlights that they create narrow perceptions about reality, which simplify and help democratise the political discourse. Chagas' idea makes sense especially if we take the growing political polarisation after 2013 and the increasing access to social media and message apps into account. The definition of a meme is rarely a consensus, but Anastasia Denisova (2019, 10) provides an accessible description that indicates that memes may have a starting point in an image or stereotype: "A meme is an imitable text that Internet users appropriate, adjust and share in the digital sphere. The initial text may be [...] any digital unit of expression, as long as it conveys certain meaning or emotion and encourages others to either add something to the content or shape". She also highlights that memes tend to change as they circulate on the internet (Denisova 2019). By analysing some of 'WhatsApp aunt' memes, we want to highlight how the original image of 'older women who share fake news' changes to convey different meanings.

The first two memes are left leaning, while the last two show how the Brazilian right appropriated the 'WhatsApp aunt' for its political propaganda. The first one is a poster that says 'Beware! Elderly confused in green and yellow' (Figure 1). The use of these colours is a reference to the colours of the Brazilian flag, and it is also an allusion to the use of the Brazil soccer jersey, which, since 2013, has become a symbol for right-wingers.

Image 1 – 'Beware! Elderly confused in green and yellow'

Doutor de Mente 2021

Image 2 – 'The aunt that spreads fake news on WhatsApp'

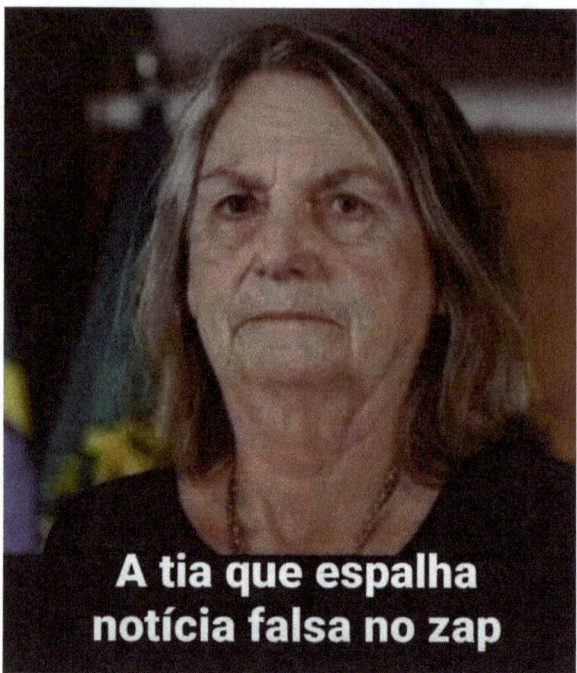

Simão 2022

The second meme (Figure 2) shows Bolsonaro portrayed as an old woman, and it reads 'The aunt that spreads fake news on WhatsApp'. This is clearly a reference to Bolsonaro's use of WhatsApp bulk senders. Both the text and the message identify Bolsonaro's pivotal role in the spread of fake news implying that it was not only old women who spread fake news. At the same time, the meme is still highly problematic as it portrays the president as an old woman. This meme combines ageism and sexism for a comic effect, implicitly relying on the widespread belief that old women should not be taken seriously in the realm of politics. That is, by presenting the president as an old woman, the meme implies that Bolsonaro should not be taken seriously because the opinions of old women are not respected.

The third meme (Figure 3) depicts a conservative old woman. The image was manipulated to add the 'thug life' glasses, a reference to a Snoop Dogg song, which often includes the soundtrack of memes that portray someone acting 'like a boss'. The text says: 'WhatsApp aunt, the terror of the left', indicating that older women act 'like bosses' because of their support.

Image 3 – 'WhatsApp aunt, the terror of the left'

Source unknown

The last meme (Figure 4) depicts an old woman using her cell phone. The text reads: 'Thank you, WhatsApp aunt, for freeing Brazil from another four years of PT's government'. Unlike the other memes, the origin of the fourth meme is clear: it stems from a politician that supports Bolsonaro. This meme also acknowledges the stereotype of old women spreading (fake) news, suggesting that these women were responsible for the election of Bolsonaro.

Image 4 – 'Thank you, WhatsApp aunt, for freeing Brazil from another four years of PT's government'

Zambelli 2018

These memes are just a few examples that showcase the use of stereotypes about older, politically engaged women. As seen in the memes, 'WhatsApp aunts' as a stereotype is used by the left and the right. The memes from the left tend to depict Bolsonaro voters as confused or gullible older women, thus using age and gender as pejorative categories. Consequently, the left denies the agency of older women, while the right celebrates these 'aunts' and grants them some political agency. Even though the right's use of stereotypes is more positive, they are still referencing a controlling image that may propel some older women to reclaim political participation. What also calls our attention is the absence of racialised people from the discourses about 'WhatsApp aunts'. In the highly inequal landscape of Brazil, racialised citizens do not have much space to articulate their opinions and are often entirely excluded from the political discourse as seen in the memes. Moreover, the stereotype and the portrayal of 'WhatsApp aunts' in the memes also points to an exclusion of poor populations, many of them racialised, who may not have access to a cell phone or social media, or even might not have learned how to read.

WhatsApp as Means to Reactivate the Agency of 'Aunts'

In a book analysing the discourses around programs for older people, Eneida G. M. Haddad (2017) studies the construal of old age in Brazil. Examining the medical discourses that justify many of these programs, Haddad recognises that they echo the capitalist idea that people are valuable as long as they work (2017, 74), hence they should remain active in old age (2017, 71). Once they retire, older people are thought to be inactive and their worth consequently diminishes (Haddad 2017, 70–71). The researcher acknowledges the class component imbued in the discourse of remaining active: it does not take into consideration members of the working class whose tired bodies may have been unwillingly deteriorated due to the constant wear and tear of work (Haddad 2017, 53) and who, in their retirement, may want to rest and/or do leisure activities. Haddad's research indicates what becomes of old people in Brazil when they retire: they are dismissed as disposable. This reality is not much different from what happens to older people elsewhere. The increasing number of older populations has prompted the discourse of the 'grey tsunami' in several contexts and publications. But what if being old and a woman can empower you?

Take the example of Lilian Gardino. She refuses to be fazed by the stereotypes used to discredit her just because she is old. Instead, she uses the 'WhatsApp aunt' epithet to reclaim her agency, feel empowered, and promote her YouTube channel. In a video posted on November 21, 2019, Gardino, a chipper old white woman, introduces herself: "I'm not a robot, I am a human in flesh and bones, OK? [...] I'm just like you on the other side of the screen. I'm neither part of the digital militia nor earn money for my engagement" (Lilian Tia do Zap 2019). She is wearing a green and yellow T-shirt that reads 'My party is Brazil', indicating that, in the highly polarised Brazilian political scenario, Gardino is right leaning. She is sitting on her living room couch and has an improvised script in her hands. For twenty minutes, she talks about herself: she is 60,[9] has two

---

9   In Brazil, old age officially starts at age 60, so, in our analysis, we comply with its current start.

children, is married, works as a public-school teacher in the state of São Paulo, does handcraft as a hobby, and often uses *Sistema Único de Saúde (SUS)*, Brazil's network of public health services. In addition to her introduction, in this video, she broaches some of the topics that she wants to debate in her YouTube channel: criticism of politicians (including the ones she voted for), abortion, religion, immigration, 'gays', and the military dictatorship, which she affirms was 'very different from what people preach' (Lilian Tia do Zap 2019). This is her second YouTube video, and the name of her channel is "Lilian Tia do Zap", a reference to the well-known figure of 'WhatsApp aunt.'

In her channel, Gardino is friendly and proud to be a 'WhatsApp aunt' because she views the negative stereotyping as an inaccurate representation of her experience and discernment, which only comes with time. 'We are aunties and uncles, we are the elderly, but we are not dumb, and people underestimate our intelligence', she vents and then mentions that she is committed to rescuing 'the values of our parents and grandparents' (Lilian Tia do Zap 2019). For these purposes, she believes it is necessary to engage in activism to free Brazil from the legacy of corruption that the left has supposedly bequeathed.

Every three to four days, Gardino uploads a new video. As promised, she comments on the latest news. Almost all videos reproduce ideas that circulate in the right-wing informative bubbles (Pariser 2011) of social media. These contents are shared by either bots or humans within polarised groups, reinforcing the members' already established perspectives and ways of thinking. This 'echo chamber' functionality of social media sharing reinforces consistent beliefs and creates the impression that 'everybody thinks like me', which, in turn, encourages even more political polarisation.

But why would someone believe in fake news? Because of the distrust in the already established media, Perini-Santos (2021, 350) emphasises that people seek alternative news sources that corroborate their world views and explains that this is a move people do to help them confirm and maintain their identities. That is, identity enables us to understand the investment of many of these 'WhatsApp aunts' in their informative bubbles. But identity does not only explain why people believe in fake news, it is also one of the main reasons someone may engage in politics in the first place. In their study of social movements, Rob Rosenthal and Richard Flacks (2012, 7) analyse why people engage in politics, when this can pose a risk to their well-being. They argue that collective and personal identities are connected to political activism in the sense that participating in a social movement enables a person to elaborate on their role in society and find fulfilment. In other words, 'WhatsApp aunt's' political participation points to an important intersection of informative bubbles, old age, and identity, indicating that political activism is an appealing alternative to those who feel disposable and marginalised.

In Gardino's case, we notice that she uses her age to emphasise her legitimacy in being politically active, but she also portrays herself in gendered terms when she claims the identity of an 'aunt' as seen in how she describes herself and in the name of her channel. That is, gender is also part of the equation that explains her political activism because as an older woman, she likely experiences more marginalisation. Einwohner, Hollander and Olson (2000, 684–690) argue that social movements are always gendered in at least one or more of their layers: composition, goals, tactics, attribution, that is, how they are seen by the public, and identity. Data shows that most of Bolsonaro's supporters tend to be older men instead of women (Lopes 2021). As for the goals, if Bolsonaro supporters are aligned with his politics (Kaiser 2018), they are likely not fighting for gender equality or any gender-related revindications. Also, going to protests and sharing (fake) news are practises that are not limited to one specific gender. The main layers that interest us are attribution and identity.

The use of 'aunt' instead of 'uncle' in the expression 'WhatsApp aunt' and the memes featuring older women highlight that the public, in general, and the left, in particular, make gendered assumptions about who is politically active online. These assumptions are highly problematic because the stereotype about older women who are politically active online points to the supposed lack of legitimacy that these women would have as a social movement. Similarly, by using the word 'aunt', the left expels old women from the public arena where politics takes place, constraining them to domesticity by identifying them in relation to a family group, outside the public space. This creates a double standard at the intersection of age and gender when it comes to how the left represents its opponents, as Bolsonaro's male supporters are not associated with the stereotype or meme. Rosenthal and Flacks (2012, 6) affirm that the success of a social movement depends on how it will present itself to the public and the consequent legitimacy that the public may or may not attribute to it. That is, the more familiar a movement frames itself, the more likely it is to be successful (Einwohner, Hollander and Olson 2000, 691). With the Brazilian left in mind, these claims are also true when it comes to the rebuttal of a political position. In face of the widespread use of the expression 'widowess of the dictatorship' discussed previously, the left's framing of politically active older women as 'WhatsApp aunts' accesses a prominent public bias that is used to disempower older women by emphasising their supposed lack of legitimacy and critical thought.

These negative attributions do not stop older women from participating in the political discourse as seen in Gardino's YouTube channel (Lilian Tia do Zap 2019). Her most eloquent moments coincide with her participation in public demonstrations in favour of Bolsonaro in the streets of São Paulo. Even during the Covid-19 pandemic, she is not afraid to go to the streets to demand the purging of the Supreme Court, the ousting of the president of the Congress, military intervention, among other revindications, all part of Bolsonaro's antidemocratic and denialist agenda. Through her actions, Gardino exercises her political and social agencies: not only does she invite her viewers to join her, but she also often goes live on YouTube reporting from the event, socialising with other protesters dressed in green and yellow, 'fangirling' other youtubers with similar political beliefs and meeting some of her followers (Lilian Tia do Zap 2019). In a 2021 video shot during Brazil's Independence Day's festivities, she is visibly enjoying herself while she sells DIY 'WhatsApp aunt's' T-shirts (Lilian Tia do Zap 2021).

For 'WhatsApp aunts', political protests are the pinnacle of their engagement because their activism happens in the abstraction of social media platforms, where people often connect with others who they may not know well, either due to a common interest, or even the hatred fuelled by the political discontentment that the circulation of fake news exacerbates. At home, in the solitude of cell phone or computer screens, their political engagement becomes crucial not only for their own artic- ulation of their identities, but as a means to survive the isolation inten- sified by the pandemic, which has occurred during most of Bolsonaro's term. Old people that are active in the (far) right are usually motivated by their outrage, which might distance them from the often projected images of wise and resilient old age. Even though political activism and protests from both left and right-wing movements are represented as an expression of outrage over oppression, triggered by injustice, in the case of old people, this outrage is misread as lack of sanity and coher- ence. Félix and Debert (2021) confirm this idea when they assert that old people's social criticism is then dismissed and diminished and often in- terpreted as a symptom of one of the pathologies that are often linked to later life (dementia, depression, etc.).

Conclusion

On January 8, 2023, following the defeat of Bolsonaro in the 2022 elec- tion, his most radical supporters invaded and vandalized the three main government buildings in Brasília, capital of Brazil: the National Congress, the Federal Supreme Court and the presidential palace. The act was a direct attack on Brazilian democracy as it intended to remove current President Lula, legitimately elected by popular vote for a new term inaugurated on January 1, 2023. While users in social media and part of the press emphasize the participation of older people by showing them in most images of the invasion that were shared and reposted, the police affirms that they arrested approximately 1,200 invaders and among them only 40 were older people (3.5%) (Caramori 2023). In fact, most of the prisoners' ages ranged mainly from 50 to 59 years old (34.5%) and 40 to 49 years old (32.6%) (Caramori 2023). That is, again, older people are the main targets of anger and mockery in connection to the invasion and one more time presumed guilty while the press attributes their supposed radicalism to advanced age. And yet the real participation of older people in this invasion (the 3.5%) still needs to be complicated and examined in terms of their motivation and identification with the stereotype and then identity of 'WhatsApp Aunts.'

However, in spite of the ongoing misinformation spread in right-leaning informative bubbles and how it is used in the construal of the 'WhatsApp aunt' stereotype and memes, we, as authors of the text, reject the beliefs that older people (and especially older women) are gullible or liable for Bolsonaro's victory in 2018 or were the main actors of the depredation that happened in Brasília in January of 2023 (as the police reports confirms). Similarly, even though we distance ourselves from positions such as Gardino's, we do not believe that her political opinion is due to her age, gender or the intersection of both. Research shows that people over 60 are only *one* of the different age groups that consistently shows support for Bolsonaro (Lopes 2021). This data highlights that, in Brazil, the spread of misinformation is connected to issues of structural inequalities due to legacies of colonisation and of consequent precarious relations with countries of the Global North. The lack of conversations about the military dictatorship and attempts to sweep this issue under the rug such as the Amnesty Law also contribute to a growing distrust in institutions which, in turn, is one of the factors that explain the enduring distribution of fake news by right-wing partisans in Brazil.

Lastly, we recognise that it is problematic to collapse all left movements under an umbrella term. In the Brazilian scenario, the lack of dialogue among different left movements is notorious and is, in part, due to the range of differences that are seemingly unbridgeable. However, one commonality between these left movements is the dismissal of age as a factor that adds to marginalisation. Having said that, it may be idealistic on our part to expect that the left starts a debate and a praxis that includes age or ageism. On the other hand, if the left who strives for social justice and change does not do it, who else will?

Acknowledgement

We thank Jessica Anne Carter for her help proofreading this chapter, the anonymous reviewers and the book editors for their valuable suggestions.

References

"Bolsonaro Celebra 'Tia Do Zap' e Deseja 'Bom Fim De Ano e Excelente 22 Para Todos Nós.'" Gazeta Do Povo, 20 December 2020. https://w ww.gazetadopovo.com.br/republica/breves/bolsonaro-celebra-tia-do-zap-e-deseja-bom-fim-de-ano-e-excelente-22-para-todos-nos/

Brum, Maurício. "Enquanto Brasil Pode Eleger Viúvas Da Ditadura, Chile Segue Punindo Seus Militares." The Intercept Brasil, 11 September 2018. https://theintercept.com/2018/09/11/brasil-viuvas-ditadur a-chile-pinochet/ (

Campos Mello, Patricia. A Máquiná do Ódio: Notas de Uma Repórter sobre Fake News e Violência Digital. São Paulo: Companhia Das Letras, 2020.

Caramori, Iana. *Idosos são 3,5% dos bolsonaristas radicais presos em Brasília, e maioria tem de 40 a 59 anos; veja lista.* G1, 12 January 2023. https://g1 .globo.com/df/distrito-federal/noticia/2023/01/12/idosos-sao-35pe rcent-dos-bolsonaristas-radicais-presos-em-brasilia-e-maioria-te m-de-40-a-59-anos-veja-lista.ghtml

Cardoso, Carlos. "Aquela Sua Tia Do WhatsApp Não É a Faca Mais Afiada Da Gaveta." Meio Bit, 7 December 2015. www1.tecnoblog.net/meio-bit/332599/estudo-canadense-aponta-pessoas-que-repassam-frases-motivacionais-no-whatsapp-podem-possuir-grave-defici-encia-intelectual

Carro, Rodrigo. "Brazil." Reuters Institute for the Study of Journalism. reutersinstitute.politics.ox.ac.uk/digital-news-report/2021/brazil

Cesarino, Letícia. "Populismo Digital: Roteiro Inicial para Um Conceito, a partir de um Estudo de Caso da Campanha Eleitoral de 2018 (Parte

I: Metodologia e Teoria)." Academia 25.1 (2021). https://bit.ly/3OHH
R04 (20 April 2022).

Chagas, Viktor. "A Febre dos Memes de Política". Revista FAMECOS 25.1
(2018). https://doi.org/10.15448/1980-3729.2018.1.27025.

Constantino, Rodrigo. "As 'Tias Do Zap' e a 'Revolução' Da Terceira
Idade." Gazeta Do Povo, 18 November 2019. https://www.gazetadop
ovo.com.br/rodrigo-constantino/as-tias-do-zap-e-a-revolucao-da
-terceira-idade/

Damgaard, Mads Bjelke. Media Leaks and Corruption in Brazil: The In-
fostorm of Impeachment and the Lava-Jato Scandal. New York: Routledge, 2019.

de Albuquerque, Afonso, and Rodrigo Quinan. "Crise epistemológica e
Teorias da conspiração: O Discurso Anti-Ciência do Canal 'Professor
Terra Plana'". Revista Mídia e Cotidiano 13.3 (2019): 83–104. https://d
oi.org/10.22409/rmc.v13i3.38088

Denisova, Anastasia. Internet Memes and Society: Social, Cultural and
Political Contexts. New York: Routledge, Taylor & Francis Group,
2019.

Doutor de Mente, Rigoli PhD [MarceloRigoli] "Eu ri alto na rua com isso."
Twitter, 9 September 2021. https://twitter.com/marcelorigoli/status
/1435978370555301891

Einwohner, Rachel L., Jocelyn A. Hollander, and Toska Olson. "Engender-
ing Social Movements: Cultural Images and Movement Dynamics".
Gender & Society 14.5 (2000): 679–699. https://doi.org/10.1177/08912
4300014005006

Félix, Jorge, and Guita G. Debert. "Adesão à Vacina Mostra Resistência
De Idosos a Negacionismo". Folha de São Paulo, 23 April 2021. https:
//www1.folha.uol.com.br/ilustrissima/2021/04/insubmissao-e-a-m
aior-sabedoria-que-os-mais-velhos-podem-deixar-aos-mais-joven
s.shtml

Fischberg, Josy. "Parentes Criam Grupos de WhatsApp para Se Mante-
rem Informados Sobre Assuntos De Família". O Globo, 25 July 2014.
https://oglobo.globo.com/economia/parentes-criam-grupos-de-w
hatsapp-para-se-manterem-informados-sobre-assuntos-de-famili
a-13371728

Haddad, Eneida G. de M. A Ideologia da Velhice. Kindle ed.: Cortez, 2017.

Hill Collins, Patricia. Black Feminist Thought: Knowledge, Consciousness, and The Politics of Empowerment. New York: Routledge, 2000.

Kaiser, Anna Jean. "Woman Who Bolsonaro Insulted: 'Our President-Elect Encourages Rape'." The Guardian, 23 December 2018. https://www.theguardian.com/world/2018/dec/23/maria-do-rosario-jair-bolsonaro-brazil-rape

Lapper, Richard. Beef, Bible and Bullets: Brazil in the Age of Bolsonaro. Manchester: Manchester UP, 2021.

Lilian Tia do Zap. "LILIAN TIA DO ZAP COM OS HIPÓCRITAS.....". YouTube, uploaded by Lilian Tia do Zap, 14. September 2019. https://www.youtube.com/watch?v=oaPbuDtvF78

Lilian Tia do Zap. "PAULISTA AGORA Pix 14991091242", YouTube, uploaded by Lilian Tia do Zap, 7. September 2021. https://www.youtube.com/watch?v=ebaZ--4hq7k&t=1188s (27 January 2021).

Lilian Tia do Zap. "PRAZER!!! TIA DO ZAP!!! SOMOS MUITAS!!!!" YouTube, uploaded by Lilian Tia do Zap, 21. November 2019. https://www.youtube.com/watch?v=IYGVBPYkMcs (27 January 2021).

Lilian Tia do Zap. "TIA DO ZAP RESPONDE RODRIGO CONSTANTINO". YouTube, uploaded by Lilian Tia do Zap, 20. November 2019. https://www.youtube.com/watch?v=4fYk36uKUPM (27 January 2021).

Lopes, Sophia. "Rejeição Ao Trabalho De Bolsonaro Vai Ao Recorde De 58%, Mostra PoderData". Poder360, 30 September 2021. https://www.poder360.com.br/poderdata/rejeicao-ao-trabalho-de-bolsonaro-vai-ao-recorde-de-58-mostra-poderdata/

Lorenz, Taylor. "'OK Boomer' Marks the End of Friendly Generational Relations." The New York Times, 29 October 2019. https://www.nytimes.com/2019/10/29/style/ok-boomer.html

Machado, Jorge, and Richard Miskolci. "Das Jornadas de Junho à Cruzada Moral: O Papel das Redes Sociais na Polarização Política Brasileira". Sociologia & Antropologia 9.3 (2019): 945–970. https://doi.org/10.1590/2238-38752019v9310

Moura, Maurício, and Juliano Corbellini. A Eleição Disruptiva: Por Que Bolsonaro Venceu. Kindle ed.: Editora Record, 2019.

"Pandemia e o Consumo De Notícias Nas Redes Sociais." Gente, 14 December 2020. https://gente.globo.com/pandemia-e-o-consumo-de-noticias-nas-redes-sociais/

Pariser, Eli. The Filter Bubble: What the Internet Is Hiding from You. London: Penguin, 2011.

Perini-Santos, Ernesto. "What Is Post-Truth? A Tentative Answer with Brazil as a Case Study." Democracy and Brazil: Collapse and Regression. Eds. Bernardo Bianchi, Jorge Chaloub, Patricia Rangel, Frieder Otto Wolf, Kindle ed.: Routledge, 2021. 340–374.

Possas, Lídia M. V. "Viuvez, Gênero e Oralidade: Recuperando os Sujeitos invisíveis nos 'Anos de Chumbo' (Brasil, 1970–1980)". História Oral 12.1-2 (2011), 28. Dec. 2011. https://doi.org/10.51880/ho.v12i1-2.165

Recuero, Raquel, Felipe Bonow Soares, Otávio Vinhas, Taiane Volcan, Gabriela Zago, Elisa Marchioro Stumpf, Paula Viegas, Luiz Ricardo Hüttner, Carolina Bonoto, Gabriela Silva, Iara Passos, Igor Salgueiro, and Giéle Sodré. "Desinformação, Mídia Social e COVID-19 No Brasil: Relatório, Resultados e Estratégias De Combate." MIDIARS, https://wp.ufpel.edu.br/midiars/files/2021/05/Desinformac%CC%A7a%CC%83o-covid-midiars-2021-1.pdf

Rosenthal, Rob, and Richard Flacks. Playing for Change: Music and Musicians in the Service of Social Movements. New York: Routledge, 2012.

Simão, Zé [simao.z] "Tia Cloroquina! Tia Inflação 10,6%! #zesimao #bandnewsfm #folhadesaopaulo". Instagram, 12 January 2022. https://www.instagram.com/p/CYoilOorq9L/

Soutto, Breno. "Redes Sociais e Online São as Maiores Fontes Para Consumo de Notícias, mas o Público Ainda Os Vêem com Desconfiança". Elife Brasil, 22 October 2021. https://elife.com.br/index.php/2021/10/22/redes-sociais-e-online-sao-as-maiores-fontes-noticias-do-pais-mas-publico-ainda-os-veem-com-desconfianca/ (27 January 2021).

Tas, Marcelo. "Patrícia Campos Mello Comenta sobre a 'Tia do Zap.'" YouTube, uploaded by Provoca. 21 October 2020. https://www.youtube.com/watch?v=YkYX6B1PWWA

Zambelli, Carla [CarlaZambelli38]. "Tia do zap: a mais nova face da 'extrema-direita' brasileira! Parabéns, tia!" Twitter, 19 October 2018. https://twitter.com/CarlaZambelli38/status/105340405689344 0000?s=20&t=Kdts-ZwfA1ZQo1qpJ8iYNw

Contributors

Leonor Acosta Bustamante, PhD, is a Permanent Lecturer in Cultural Studies and Gender Studies at the Department of Modern Languages at the University of Cadiz. Her research interests in the crossing of gender traits and the deconstruction of gender binaries have recently expanded towards the analysis of ageing masculinities in films and literature. She has recently published a number of book chapters and indexed articles dealing with age and gender, such as "Disabled Masculinity as a Metaphor of National Conflict in the Cold War era: Orson Welles' *The Lady form Shanghai*" (2019), and "Reconstructing the (Masculine) Self from Old Age: Memories of the Aching Male Body in Paul Auster's *Winter Journal*" (2021). She is currently an active member of several international networks researching gender, sexuality, and transfeminism, some of them established in South America, and works as a referee for several journals and institutional publishing groups.

Shlomit Aharoni Lir is a postdoctoral researcher at Bar Ilan University. She focuses her research on the intersections of gender, technology and media. She is particularly interested in how marginalized social groups are depicted in cultural and digital spheres. Her research includes the exploration and theorization of cultural aspects of Israeli society, as well as gendered aspects of the cinematic world and civic society in the digital era. Among the numerous awards she has received is the prestigious Golda Meir Postdoctoral Award for the Advancement of Women in Science and Technology, from the Israeli Ministry of Innovation, Science and Technology. Aharoni Lir is a social entrepreneur and the founder of Women Activists Online, a hub initiative designed to promote women leadership through social media. She is an accomplished writer, who writes on issues concerning social justice, inclusion, diversity, and women's rights. Among the books she published are Spreading Wings, the Feminist Haggadah and In Visible Ink.

Liat Ayalon is a researcher in the School of Social Work, at Bar Ilan University, Israel. Prof. Ayalon seeks to promote awareness of ageism, in order to create change at the political and social levels. She was a core group member of the World Health Organization (WHO) global campaign to counter ageism and is one of the SAPEA work group members responsible for the report concerning the future of ageing, which was produced for the European Commission. At Bar-Ilan, she directs a research lab on psychosocial aspects of ageing and heads the Impact Center for the study of ageism and old age. Her research focuses on the interface between formal caregiving and informal care provided by family and friends for older people, and on ageism. Prof. Ayalon completed her PhD in Clinical Psychology at the Illinois Institute of Technology and pre- and post-doctoral training at the University of California, San Francisco (UCSF). She has published over 250 articles in leading journals. She is the recipient of several international awards, served as the coordinator of a Ph.D. program on the topic of ageism (Euroageism.eu) and the chair of a COST Action on the topic of ageism (IS1402). She was recently selected by the UN Decade of Healthy Ageing as one of 50 world leaders working to transform the world to be a better place in which to grow older.

Mariana Castelli-Rosa is a PhD student (Cultural Studies) at Trent University, Canada. She has a two Mas (English Studies from the University of Heidelberg, Germany and Public Texts from Trent University, Canada) and a BA in English and Portuguese (University of São Paulo, Brazil). Her areas of interest are Canadian and Indigenous literatures, identity, marginalized communities, aging, intercultural communication and translation. She works as a Research Assistant editing and annotating through coding the journal PK Page wrote during her time in Brazil.

Her doctoral research is on the experience of aging in Indigenous communities in Canada through the analysis of works of life writing and novels.

Karen Fournier is an Associate Professor of Music Theory at the School of Music, Theatre, and Dance at the University of Michigan. Her research focuses principally on issues of gender, sexuality, and class through published work on British and American punk rock in the 1970s. She is currently completing a book-length project on women's expressions of sexism and classism through punk. Karen has also published the first book-length scholarly study of Alanis Morissette's work, *The Words and Music of Alanis Morissette* (2015), where she examines the artist's contributions to the "angry young woman" phenomenon of the early 1990s. Building on her interest in Morissette's feminism, Karen explores some of Morissette's more recent work in this essay.

Nicole Haring is a PhD candidate at the Center for Inter-American Studies of the University of Graz, Austria. Her research interests focus on feminist theory, gender studies, ageing studies, and education. She received a Fulbright Scholarship in 2019/20 to teach and study at the University of Oklahoma and the Elisabeth-List Fellowship for Gender Studies from the University of Graz in 2020/21. Currently, she is working on her dissertation on intergenerational storytelling as a recipient of the doctorial fellowship from the Austrian Academy of Science. She has been a researcher in the MascAge project (www.mascage.eu) working on masculinities and ageing, as well as in the Erasmus+ project DigLit (www.diglit.eu), working on Young Adult Literature and Digital Storytelling.

Isabella Hesse is completing a Master of Arts degree in European Ethnology at the University of Vienna. Her research interests include gender, queerness, sexuality, and popular culture, with a focus on fan studies and intersectional feminism. She is currently conducting ethnographic research on boundary setting among strip club dancers. Hesse holds a scholarship from the German Academic Scholarship Foundation. After completing a Bachelor of Arts degree in Cultural Anthropology and European Ethnology at the Albert-Ludwigs-University of Freiburg, she now lives in Vienna.

Mariana Lins is a PhD candidate in Communication at the Federal University of Pernambuco (Brazil). She is a journalist and has a MA in Communication. Her work focuses specifically on ageism in the music industry and her current project is about female aging as a nuisance in pop music. Lins is mainly interested in gender studies, pop culture, media and performance studies. During 2019–2020, received a scholarship from the Brazilian Coordination for the Improvement of Higher Education Personnel (Capes) to join a doctoral exchange program at the University of Oviedo (Spain). She is also part of the scientific committee of the Popfilia Symposium, held by the Federal University of Pernambuco, and one of the editors of the book *Divas Pop – O Corpo-Som das Cantoras na Cultura Midiática* (PPGCOM-UFMG, 2021).

Roberta Maierhofer is professor of American Studies and director of the Center for Inter-American Studies at the University of Graz, Austria. Her research interests focus on aging studies, feminist theory, gender studies, and inter-cultural and transnational education. Currently, she is the PI of the Austrian team of the MascAge (www.mascage.eu) project and the PI of the Erasmus+ project DigLit (www.diglit.eu). In the 1990s, she developed the approach of anocriticism that focuses on the intersections of gender and age. She is a founding member of the European Network of Aging Studies and a leading expert in the field. Her monograph *Salty Old Women- Frauen, Altern, und Identität in der amerkanischen Literatur und Kultur* was among the first works that analyzed the intersections of gender and aging in American literature and culture. Her recent publications focus on intergenerationality and aging masculinities.

Raquel Medina is a Visiting Research Fellow at Aston University, UK. Her current research focuses on cultural representations of dementia. She is the author of *Cinematic Representations of Alzheimer's Disease* (Palgrave, 2018), a monograph that provides an in-depth analysis of non-mainstream films across cultures dealing with dementia/AD as their main topic. Medina is co-director *Dementia and Cultural Narrative Network*, *Director of the International Research Network CinemAGEnder*, and Executive Director of the *European Network in Aging Studies* (ENAS).

After living in Ireland and working as a freelance EFL teacher, **Melinda Niehus-Kettler** studied English & American Studies as well as Jewish Studies. She took a special interest in body, gender, and postcolonial studies and finished her master's course on Anglophone Literature and Culture in 2019. The PhD candidate researches on embodied power structures, (trans- and intergenerational) patterns of violence and forms of resistance. Recent projects include the chapters "Becoming One of the Others" in Ageing Masculinities, Alzheimer's and Dementia Narratives (edited by Heike Hartung, Rüdiger Kunow, and Matthew Sweney; Bloomsbury, 2022) and "Naturalising Perceived Otherness: Embodied Patterns of Violence" in Geschlechter in Un-Ordnung: Wissenschaftliche Irritationen binärer Geschlechterkonstruktionen (edited by Nina Hackmann, Dulguun Shirchinbal, and Christina Wolff; Verlag Barbara Budrich, forthcoming).

Barbara Ratzenböck is a sociologist and Senior Scientist at the Center for Inter-American Studies of the University of Graz. Her research and teaching focus on digitalization, gender, and generations, as well as Inter-American studies. She is currently a co-investigator of the international research project 'Aging in Data' (SSHRC Canada, PI: Kim Sawchuk, Concordia University). She has also been actively involved in the project Ageing + Communication + Technologies, among others as dataset coordinator of the Austrian survey of the Cross-national Longitudinal Study: Older Audiences in the Digital Media Environment. She has published on media generations, older women's ICT use, and recently on aging masculinities. Recently, she has received the ENAS (European Network of Aging Studies) award for best dissertations for her PhD thesis on older women's ICT use in Austria.

Acknowledgments

The editors would like to acknowledge the *Elisabeth-List-Fellowship Programme for Gender Studies* at the University of Graz for the financial contribution to the project "Gender and Age/ing in Popular Culture – Particularly in Music" which made this publication possible and where all editors were involved in. Furthermore, we would like to acknowledge the *Sector Science and Research* (Abteilung 12: *Wissenschaft & Forschung*) of the *County Styria* for their financial support. We would also like to acknowledge the ERA Gender-Net+ research project *MASCAGE – Analyzing Social Constructions of Ageing Masculinities and their Cultural Representations in Contemporary European Literatures and Cinemas* whose researchers have contributed to this volume. This research was funded in part by the Austrian Science Fund (FWF) [I4187]. We would also like to give special thanks to Lea Pešec and Eva Bauer for their valuable proof reading. To the reviewers, who generously provided us with their expertise and made this publication possible, we extend our gratitude. Finally, we would like to thank the authors in this book who embarked on this adventure. Thank you for your contribution and for being part of this project.

Kulturwissenschaft

Tobias Leenaert
Der Weg zur veganen Welt
Ein pragmatischer Leitfaden

2022, 232 S., kart., 18 SW-Abbildungen
20,00 € (DE), 978-3-8376-5161-4
E-Book:
PDF: 17,99 € (DE), ISBN 978-3-8394-5161-8
EPUB: 17,99 € (DE), ISBN 978-3-7328-5161-4

Markus Gabriel, Christoph Horn, Anna Katsman, Wilhelm Krull,
Anna Luisa Lippold, Corine Pelluchon, Ingo Venzke
Towards a New Enlightenment –
The Case for Future-Oriented Humanities

2022, 80 p., pb.
18,00 € (DE), 978-3-8376-6570-3
E-Book: available as free open access publication
PDF: ISBN 978-3-8394-6570-7
ISBN 978-3-7328-6570-3

Marc Dietrich, Martin Seeliger (Hg.)
Deutscher Gangsta-Rap III
Soziale Konflikte und kulturelle Repräsentationen

2022, 378 S., kart., 2 Farbabbildungen
35,00 € (DE), 978-3-8376-6055-5
E-Book:
PDF: 34,99 € (DE), ISBN 978-3-8394-6055-9

Kulturwissenschaft

Michael Thompson
Mülltheorie
Über die Schaffung und Vernichtung von Werten

2021, 324 S., kart., 57 SW-Abbildungen
27,00 € (DE), 978-3-8376-5224-6
E-Book:
PDF: 23,99 € (DE), ISBN 978-3-8394-5224-0
EPUB: 23,99 € (DE), ISBN 978-3-7328-5224-6

Thomas Hecken, Moritz Baßler, Elena Beregow,
Robin Curtis, Heinz Drügh, Mascha Jacobs,
Annekathrin Kohout, Nicolas Pethes, Miriam Zeh (Hg.)
POP
Kultur und Kritik (Jg. 11, 2/2022)

2022, 180 S., kart.
16,80 € (DE), 978-3-8376-5897-2
E-Book:
PDF: 16,80 € (DE), ISBN 978-3-8394-5897-6

Eva Blome, Moritz Ege, Maren Möhring,
Maren Lickhardt, Heide Volkening (Hg.)
»Süüüüß!«
Zeitschrift für Kulturwissenschaften, Heft 1/2022

2022, 128 S., kart., 5 Farbabbildungen
14,99 € (DE), 978-3-8376-5898-9
E-Book:
PDF: 14,99 € (DE), ISBN 978-3-8394-5898-3

GPSR Authorized Representative: Easy Access System Europe, Mustamäe tee 50, 10621 Tallinn, Estonia, gpsr.requests@easproject.com

www.ingramcontent.com/pod-product-compliance
Lightning Source LLC
Chambersburg PA
CBHW061751120626
46550CB00005B/1960